faith
under
fire

faith
under
fire

Testimonies of
Christian Bravery

Collected by
Antoine Rutayisire

Edited by Anne Coomes

AFRICAN ENTERPRISE

Published by African Enterprise, Victoria House, Victoria
Road, Buckhurst Hill, Essex IG9 5EX

Reprinted 1998, 2007

ISBN 978-0-9529312-0-1

Scripture quotations are taken from: New International
Version
© 1973, 1978, 1984 International Bible Society.

British Library Cataloguing in Publication Data.
A catalogue record for this book is available from the
British Library.

Printed in England.

*Dedicated to
Israel, a man who lived what
he preached, who was gunned
down the very first day
the massacres began.*

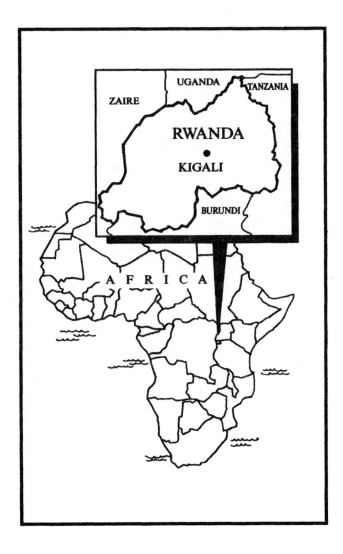

Contents

*These testimonies were all
given by the people concerned
and are written in their own words.*

Foreword

On 6 April 1994 President Habyarimana of Rwanda was killed when his plane was shot down over Kigali, captial of Rwanda. The assassination sparked off the greatest genocide Rwanda has ever known.

In the months that followed, between half a million to one million people were massacred. Two million fled and became refugees. One million were displaced within the country.

The genocide was based on the ethnic hatred between the two main groups in Rwanda, the Hutu and the Tutsi. President Habyarimana was a Hutu, and his murder, in a country already politically tense, became an excuse for Hutu extremists to unleash their killing machine. The Tutsi, as well as some opposition Hutu groups, became the target.

Before the massacres, no one would have believed that such a thing could happen in a country like Rwanda. Tucked just south of Uganda, west of Tanzania, north of Burundi and east of Zaire, this beautiful green and hilly land was considered one of the most Christian in Africa, with 90% of the population calling themselves either Roman Catholic or Protestant.

However, not all the Christians turned to violence. As the following stories show.

Some terms are used in the following pages. This is what they mean:

RPF (Rwanda Patriotic Front) – made up of Tutsis in exile

Interahamwe militias – Hutu extremists who were killers

Government soldiers – Hutu soldiers in the Rwanda army

For a fuller explanation of the Rwanda tragedy, please see the last two chapters at the back of this book.

Introduction from Antoine

By Antoine Rutayisire

The idea of collecting stories of Christian deeds during the 1994 massacres in Rwanda first came into my mind one Sunday while in the camp in Byumba.

The service that day was especially rich in testimonies of how good the Lord had been to so many. One testimony struck me by its originality and depth. A lady, Rosalie, was brought in the church on crutches. Her face and in fact her whole body, was still wrapped up in white bandages. Her neck was held in position by a special plaster collar. Wherever I looked at her, I felt deep pity .

Then in the middle of the service she stood up and asked if she, too, could give a short testimony. I was expecting a tirade of self-pity and accusations, a recounting of all the suffering and misery she had gone through. I expected her to want to arouse sympathy for herself and anger at the criminals who had reduced her to that state. But Rosalie astonished all of us by the positive praise she gave to the Lord. She told the assembly how the Interahamwe had captured her, had killed all her family, and then had cut her in all deadly places. They cut her temples, her neck, and all over the body. She was left to die on the border of the road.

For three days she bled and suffered pain from the cuts, thirst and cold under the heavy rains. Finally she was found by the RPF soldiers who gave her first aid treatment and then transferred her to the hospital. She recounted her story in a factual manner, without any attempt to create emotional effect, and praising the Lord for every detail of her rescue.

The conclusion was more powerful than the story. 'I know all the people who did this to me. They were our immediate neighbours. I spoke to them and they gave me time to pray for them before they started cutting me and I prayed for them until I lost consciousness. I forgave them before they did it and I still feel forgiveness for them. If I were to meet them even today, I would not hand them over to justice. I have forgiven them and I wish them well. I know it was the devil that led them to do such an abomination, and I pray the Lord to save their souls from perdition.'

Considering the state she was in, the testimony was so powerful. I was later to hear more, similar, testimonies of Christians who died praying for their killers and even calling them to repentance. Very unfortunately, we have not been able to collect detailed testimonies of this type, as the people who would have given them to us are dead.

The testimonies in this book came to us – obviously – through the survivors. Many of these witnessed horrific scenes of killing, many overheard the killers feeling remorse after killing such people.

The danger in a collection of this nature is that the survivors seem to be the successful ones. Indeed they are fortunate – but we believe that in Christ those who died a brave and forgiving death are just as successful. Christians are called to witness to Christ, and whether they live or die, if they do so, then they have not died in vain.

This collection is full of praise for God's care and protection for those who survived. But the survivors would also thank God that the Christians who died were given grace and courage to die...

After the genocide came the critical attacks on the Church in Rwanda. She was blamed for failing to stop the massacres. It sounded as if all the Christians had failed. And it sounded as if all Bahutu were criminals and extremists. This did not do justice to many individual Christians who took heroic positions and protected their neighbours, often at the risk of their own lives. Such deeds of bravery would go unnoticed if nobody took pains to collect them.

People have been asking for this to be done, like this excerpt from a conference:

'...although the Church as an institution failed, there are testimonies of individual Christians and Christian initiative groups that helped to save lives or even gave their lives for others. Nobody talks much about them. But their great testimonies should be collected, written and published. They are the hope of the country, because those Christians overcame the barriers of hatred and ethnic divisions.' (The Rev. Malachie Munyaneza, quoted by Michael Cassidy)

The same type of appeal was made by Roger Bowen in a J.C.Jones Lecture 1995

'The challenge to find a deeper, more fundamental identity "in Christ", where there is no Jew nor Greek, Hutu nor Tutsi, seems to have been forgotten by many. There were glorious exceptions to this, and the stories have yet to be told, of heroic faith and courage where Christians who were also Hutu helped and protected their Tutsi neighbours from the Interahamwe militias.'

The idea of responding to such appeals, and producing a collection of stories was greeted enthusiastically by our African Enterprise Team. Particularly because our own team leader in Rwanda, Israel Havugimana, and his family, died in the massacres.

Israel was a man who lived what he preached... and he preached against ethnic hatred. In the 1972/73 massacres he had protected a Mututsi fellow student at Shyogwe Secondary school, covering him with his own body and receiving all the beating until he managed to get him out of the reach of the attackers.

During the 1990-1994 tensions that led to the genocide, Israel stayed equal to his Christian commitment, spearheading a reconciliation ministry through a nationwide city crusade. But his friendship with Tutsi brothers and sisters was resented by the extemists, and the Bible study group that met at his home was mistaken for RPF support meetings. In February 1994 a handgrenade was thrown into his home as a warning. We then discussed the possibility of stopping our prayer group, so as not to compromise him any longer.

'What Christian testimony would that be?' he retorted. 'To shy away from my brothers and sisters because they are targetted! I have been preaching reconciliation, and I will live it even if I have to pay for it with my own blood.'

Pay with his blood he did. He was gunned down the very first day of the massacres with his three daughters, Rachel, Danielle and Mireille, in the company of his father and some visitors. (Danielle survived the wounds and is alive.)

This collection of testimonies, then, is dedicated to Israel's memory.

African Enterprise – Rwanda wants to thank Otto Harold of the Mennonite Central Committee, who funded its research by sending a staffworker on tour of the whole of Rwanda to seek out Christians with stories to tell. More than 40 pastors and lay people talked, though it was not always easy for them to recall such horrific experiences. Some testimonies are therefore rather short and matter of fact. Others felt a release by reliving their experiences in more dramatic emotional details.

Let this short collection be a witness that the Lord has still faithful servants, who in dire circumstances, under the threat of death, have refused to bow their knees to the bloody idol of ethnicity. Let it be a testimony of hope for a future when Rwanda will be populated by people who see each other as all created in the image of God, a time when no one will be humiliated, rejected, hated or even killed for whatever group he might be from. Let this be a testimony to the faithfulness of God.

1 Murder in the Church

Why have you rejected us forever , O God?...
Turn your steps towards these everlasting ruins,
All this destruction the enemy has brought on the
sanctuary...
They burned your sanctuary to the ground;
They defiled the dwelling place of your Name.
They said in their hearts, 'We will crush them
completely!'
They burned every place where God was
worshipped in the land.   Psalm 74:1,3,7,8

Rukara
Commune Rukara, Kibungo Prefecture.
8 April, 1994
*Told by Therese Mukamisha with additional details
from Samuel Karugende, both survivors from Rukara.*

The radio broadcast non-stop from the night of
Wednesday 6 April that the plane of President
Habyarimana had been shot and had crashed in
flames onto the runway of Kanombe Airport, outside Kigali, the capital.

The announcement was followed by orders that
nobody should move from their home. This was a
bad omen, but we did not really know what to expect.

Throughout Thursday, 7 April, our family talked
about the assassination. To us then, it was just

another dead V.I.P. There had been several others in previous months. We did not know this was going to become the worst tragedy this country has ever known..

The next afternoon, Friday, I set off, as usual, for the weekly prayer meeting at church. I never arrived. On the way I met a man coming from Gahini, who told me violence had broken out, and that houses were being burnt. Alarmed, I turned back for home, and on the way I met people who were running away in total panic.

In the short time it took me to get home, I found all the other members of my family had already fled. Everybody was heading for the Karubamba Roman Catholic parish compound. So I immediately set out with a crowd of fugitives, which was already growing large. We met some members of the Interahamwe militia, but they did not have weapons. They nevertheless stopped us and forced us to hand them all the money we had. We finally managed to get safely to the parish compound. An even larger crowd of many hundreds was already there.

On Saturday, Father Francis, a white missionary and curate of the parish, tried to organise food for all us fugitives. Those who had lived nearby agreed to go back to their fields to fetch food. When water became scarce, the head of the commune intervened and helped us to get some more. Things were still seemingly normal, by Rwandan standards. We were refugees at the parish compound, and this was not the first time such a thing had happened. We expected this would go on for some days and then we hoped to return to our homes, as we had in previous times.

But as the day wore on, things went from bad to

worse. Interahamwe militiamen were patrolling around the parish, menacing Father Francis. He finally felt so threatened that he stopped the food distributions.

Then on Sunday 10th April, the Interahamwe pulled some 15 people from our midst and killed them outside the compound. The men among us tried to defend us all by throwing stones at those Interahamwe who returned to the attack. The tension increased by the hour, until on the evening of Monday 11th the Interahamwe came back, better armed with stones, hand grenades and guns.

They assaulted the church buildings where we had taken refuge. They threw grenades through the windows into our midst and fired their guns at those who tried to escape. We did not have any protection against them and they spent all the night attacking us. Many people died during those hours of darkness.

When the sun rose, the Interahamwe came back to finish off those of us who were still alive – particularly those who had taken refuge in the church, because the door had been impossible to break down during the night. But they tried in vain, as the men inside the building stood behind the door and barricaded it with all their might. The Interahamwe continued to throw hand grenades and stones through the windows. Then they poured a jerry can of petrol into the catechism classroom, threw in a match and the fire caught in the mattresses people had brought with them. The heart-rending wailings and groanings of those dying in the fierce flames could be heard even from far away.

The killings went on all that week. The compound was under siege and continual attack. Then on the Friday a military vehicle arrived at the compound. It was full of soldiers. They asked us to open the door of the church and we briefly did so, because there was no chance of more resistance. The soldiers warned the Interahamwe that the RPF were getting near, and that they had to be fast with the job of killing the rest of us. The easiest way , they said, was to use petrol to set the whole building on fire – with all the people inside. So the Interahamwe searched for petrol – but very fortunately they did not find any handy. Some immediately returned to wounding and killing any of us they could get hold of. Others, fortunately, paused to go and slaughter some cows, and this diverted their attention from killing us. The sun went down while they were still busy with their dirty job.

When the following morning we saw a new convoy of soldiers pulling up outside the compound, we despaired of surviving. But to our great surprise, they came with compassion, asking for information, and reassuring us. We learned these were not government soldiers but the RPF. They evacuated those of us who remained – only about 300 – from the compound and led us to Gahini. We stayed there under their protection until the end of the war.

Nyange
Commune Kivumu, Prefecture Kibuye.
Told by an unnamed survivor, who was not in the church.

On Tuesday 12th April the local administrative officers (conseillers of the sectors) came around, telling the Batutsi from communes Kivumu and Bwakira that they should take refuge in the church at Nyange Parish.

The Batutsi obeyed. Even those who had been hiding in neighbours' houses and in the bushes round about came out and joined the others, thinking this would be as it had always been in the past. It was well known that all those who had taken refuge in church premises in previous massacres had never been bothered. The church had always been a safe refuge for those who succeeded in getting there.

So people flocked to the place in multitudes, and all the church compound was overcrowded. Only one priest was around. The other, Father Straton, who was usually in charge of the parish, had run away towards Nyundo and from there to Zaire.

Several days later a small number of government soldiers arrived, accompanied by the Interahamwe. They threw hand grenades, and shot into the crowd in the compound. People fled into the church building and barricaded all the doors with the church benches. The killers threw hand grenades into the church, and shot through holes wherever they could; but as there were so many people, not all of them died.

Then one of the leaders of the Interahamwe, a very wealthy businessman who lived in Kigali, advised his men to fetch bulldozers and pull down the whole building. One machine was brought from the Astaldi road building company and it was first used to cut a big hole in the front wall, breaking the wall and the main door. Then the Interahamwe entered the building and started killing.

They killed, killed and killed all day long while at the same time the machine was destroying the building. When night came they stopped and went to rest. The following day, they came with another bulldozer, shook the big building from the four corners and crashed it down on those who were left inside.

The debris, mixed with corpses, was then shovelled into the high mound that can be seen even now next to the place where the church used to stand.

We have not managed to bury the bones properly as they are doing elsewhere, as they are so mixed up with the debris. The very few people who escaped from the church fled for refuge to the neighbouring houses. But most of those were soon hunted out and killed. Probably less than ten in all survived the killings in the church at Nyange.

Mukarange
Muhazi Commune, Kibungo Prefecture
Told by an unnamed survivor.

All we Batutsi in the parish took refuge in the church compound when we saw the situation growing bad. Many people had been killed, their homes looted and set on fire. Then the Interahamwe militia came and attacked us, but we defended ourselves.

The women and children collected stones and bricks, and the men kept guard by throwing the projectiles at any who tried to get near. This did not go on for long though, because the gendarmes (armed security police) soon arrived and strengthened the assailants by using guns and hand grenades.

When the priest, Father John Bosco Munyaneza, saw the situation becoming hopeless, he decided to read the Mass and to baptise the young children as well as those who had never been baptised. In the meantime, the resistance was getting weaker and weaker as more people were getting killed.

Finally the soldiers and the Interahamwe

shouted to us that that those who had money should come out. Some decided to risk it. But they were only taken to the other side of the compound, stripped of all their money and valuables and killed on the spot. Soon after that the Interahamwe asked Father Bosco to leave the place – he was a Muhutu and the militia did not want to kill him. They begged him but he was adamant. 'These are sheep the Lord has given me to shepherd. If they must die, let me die with them. And if you want to save my life, save theirs with mine.' The Interahamwe, angered by his stubborness, backed away from the church and threw a hand grenade.

It injured many people. I was wounded on the leg and Father Bosco was also seriously wounded, but he did not immediately die. Then the Interahamwe broke into the church and started finishing off all the wounded. Those of us who still could, scrambled out and hid in the bushes around.

2 Face to Face With Death – Antoine Rutayisire

Very often people have asked me how you feel when death looks you in the eyes. Very simple: when you are well in Jesus, you feel a peace beyond all understanding and description.

On 7 April, 1994, at 1 a.m. my family was woken up by the noise of gun shots coming from the hill in front of our residence in Kigali. I slipped out of bed, went to the window and watched as the sky grew red from the exchange of bullets.

'I guess war has broken out between the RPF contingent and the Republican Guards,' I told my wife, who was panicking. By now isolated sporadic gun shots could be heard from other strategic points of Kigali, particularly in the eastern part of town, near Kanombe Airport. Later on we learned that people were being gunned down by the presidential guards on rampage all over the area.

Meanwhile, after a time, we went back to bed. We were frightened and also puzzled, not really sure of what had just happened. Was it the start of all-out war or another short-lived confrontation? No one could tell, as the tension in town had increased alarmingly since the complications in setting up the transition government – fruit of the Arusha Agreement. Violence had become part of daily life and people were murdered on the streets and even in

24

their homes without any investigations afterwards. Armed militiamen, mainly from the youth wing of the MRND, were 'kings of the streets', killing and robbing with impunity. Hand grenades had been exploding everywhere, particularly in areas of the city where opposition party members or Tutsi people met to drink. The death toll had been quite high the weeks before the fateful day. 'When is this violence going to end?,' we wondered as we sat in the bed , not knowing exactly what to do.

We had got into the habit of spending at least two hours in prayer at home each evening, pleading with the Lord for the security of the country, and for various friends in different parts of Kigali, particularly where the Interahamwe had lately been most active. We called our prayers 'Operation Standing in the Gap' after the prophecy in Ezekiel 22:30, and these times brought us nearer to the Lord and strengthened our trust in him for protection.

We took some more time to pray again before going back to sleep that night the gunfire woke us. I always praise the Lord for the wonderful blessing of deep, sound sleep even in times of trouble.

I woke just before dawn. I had been invited by the Anglican Diocese of Shyogwe to preach in a pastors' retreat that day, and wondered if I could still make it. By then the heavy gunfire had ended, though sporadic firing could be heard throughout the city. I turned on the radio to catch the morning news, but instead there was only slow, mournful classical music.

I waited in apprehension. Then came the announcement: 'The Ministry of Defence has the sorrowful duty to announce that the plane of his Excellency the President of the Republic has been shot The President died in the accident with all his company, among them the President of Burundi. Everybody is asked to stay home until further notice.'

I shuddered. 'This is big trouble,' I told my wife. I feared our world was about to fall apart. I even went outside, just to make sure the sun had risen as usual! Everything else in our lives felt so threatened. Our housemaid, Beatrice, was already up and sweeping in the backyard, helped by her younger sister, Donata. Dinah, my wife's younger sister, was cleaning dishes in the kitchen while Jeremiah, my wife's cousin, was in front of the house watching what was happening.

I stood in my backyard and called to our next door neighbour. He was standing behind his house, taking long drags at his cigarette, looking upset and nervous.

'Good morning,' I greeted him.

Silence. I repeated the greeting, thinking he had not heard me.

The only answer I got was his grumbled: 'Haven't you heard what happened?'

'Yes, I have,' I replied, suddenly not sure what to say. I waited for more from him.

'Hum, hum,' he cleared his throat and spat. 'How could such a thing be avoided when the enemies are all around us,' he said at last, making a circular gesture with his arm as if to say his house was truly surrounded by enemies. The gesture included my home – at least that is how I interpreted it.

'Do you know who did it?,' I asked with some feigned innocence. I was interested – if apprehensive – as to what he might say.

'Who needs to be told? It is the RPF and their Tutsi accomplices. And they are *everywhere*,' he said darkly, without further comment. He dropped the cigarette butt to the ground, crushed it, and hurried back into the house. Some minutes later, he came out with a machete and went away, avoiding my eye.

I stood outside musing for a while, my thoughts a whirl of confusion and deep concern. Then I went back in, found my wife in our bedroom, and reported the short conversation I'd had with our neigbour. We sat on the bed, not knowing what to do next. It was around 7:30 a.m. and we decided it was best to pray, and then to wait and see.

All of a sudden Jeremiah called us to come out quickly and see. We ignored the call and went on with our intercession. His shouts became more pressing. We shortened our prayers and went out to the front of the house. He was pointing at the Hotel Chez Lando, a short distance from our home. People were running in all directions carrying things, hiding them and going back for more. Then we saw smoke coming from the hotel. It was on fire.

Some minutes later, the sons of our neighbour returned, carrying some things they had looted, obviously from the hotel. They were full of news of the death of some of the local people, and said road blocks had been thrown up in all the streets, and that the Interahamwe were controlling all movements.

This sounded very serious indeed, and in our hearts we panicked. We went into the living room and spontaneously started our prayers again, pleading with God for our own safety and the security of our friends around the country.

Soon the noises next door grew louder. We could hear our neighbour's sons recounting the deaths of different neighbours again and again to each other. The morning dragged on, and we simply did not know what to expect. We had no thought for any household chores, and finally just sat in the house, not even talking to each other. Through the front windows we could see dust rising everytime a shell hit the concrete wall of the Palace of the National Assembly, where the RPF contingent and their leaders were housed. We pitied them and wondered if any would survive. That was the only distraction we had – that and the continuing excited chatter of the young men next door.

Around 3:30 p.m. we heard much shouting and clamour. It grew nearer and nearer to our home. Peninah was in the bedroom breastfeeding Deborah, our young daughter, who was the only person who seemed to enjoy the loud noise of blasting shells. Beatrice and Donata were in the kitchen while Jeremiah and Dinah were in another room where I had confined them, because every time they looked out they tended to become more panicky.

I looked through the window and saw a group of Interahamwe just outside the fence of our compound. They were discussing whether to first throw a hand grenade into the compound or just to break in.

'This is our turn,' I told myself. Immediately wild and weird thoughts whirled in my mind at a flashing speed. 'Am I going to let them rape my wife, kill my child and all these young women and men in my home under my very eyes without even some attempt to protect them? What type of death are we going to die? Are they going to shoot us or to cut us into pieces?' I shuddered.

Then the idea crossed my mind: 'Why don't you grab a stick or any other weapon at hand and go out and fight them? Can't you die like a man?' This was a spontaneous, human reaction. I could recognise my old self surging up, as in the past I would never have tolerated any ill-treatment without some reaction.

28

Old memories from my schooldays flashed back in my mind, such as when we had stood face to face with other students, ready to fight our way out during the 1973 Tutsi massacres.

Our resistance was rewarded then, but this time something was missing. It wasn't just that I was on my own. It was that I no longer had the inner will to fight. Then I remembered the promises the Lord had given us during our morning prayers: 'He who dwells in the shelter of the Most High will rest in the shadow of the Almighty...I will say of the Lord, He is my refuge and my fortress, my God in whom I trust.' (Psalm 91:1-2).

I remembered other Bible verses that the Lord had given us the previous week, when I had to go preaching on one retreat, and violence broke out while I was on the way: 'Have mercy on me, O God, have mercy on me, for in you my soul takes refuge. I will take refuge in the shadow of your wings until the disaster has passed.' (Psalm 57:1). Then I felt my spirit growing calmer, and I heard a quiet voice inside, telling me: 'You have been preaching sermons on loving and praying for your enemies and now you want to die shedding blood. Instead of trying to "die like a man", why don't you just "die like a Christian"?'

I was then deeply convicted in my heart as I remembered all the past efforts I had made to keep my heart pure of anger and bitterness. So I made this short prayer of confession: 'Lord, forgive me for thinking of making my own defence and give me grace to obey you even unto death. I ask for your blessing on these people, and if it is your will that we die, have them give me time to die praying for them, as You did on the cross.'

At that very moment, a feeling of deep peace that I had never experienced before flooded through me, and I felt so light inside that a breeze could have swept me off the ground. I had accepted death, and I knew what I would do when the killers came. Everything else did not matter anymore. I was ready to face death with a Christlike attitude, and I was even curious to know how it feels after death.

But I didn't find out that day, as no sooner had I finished sorting myself out inside than the staccato of a machine gun echoed down the street. 'The *inyenzi*!' – ('cockroaches' – a derisive nickname for RPF soldiers) shouted the Interahamwe, and they scattered across our compound, and ran away downhill.

I never saw those 'liberators', as I just sat where I was, still badly shaken by the whole experience. It had all lasted less than five minutes, but it felt like a lifetime... The following days would be filled with horrendous scenes, but this episode was an invaluable preparation for the traumatic events we were going to have to face. That peace and that spirit of forgiveness stayed with me even when I heard of the death of relatives and of many close friends. It comforted me on the tiring road to exile, and strengthened me through the hardships and poverty of life in a displaced persons camp.

Such a close encounter with death gave me a new understanding, a new personalised interpretation of the prophet's words:

> I will ransom them from the power of the grave,
> I will redeem them from death.
> Where, O death, are your plagues?
> Where, O grave, is your destruction?
>
> Hosea 13:14

3 The Church that Stood Together and Survived

From Pastor Mathias Bimenyimana, with additional details from other people who were also at the site.

People began arriving at our church compound on 11 April, four days after the death of President Habyarimana.

The killings had started almost at once, but people had hesitated to run away because the order had been given to stay at home. Eventually the desperate situation drove people to break the injunction, and some started fleeing to the Gakinjiro Pentecostal church compound. They came in small groups. Some were from the battlefront that was advancing from the north, others came running away from the massacres. They arrived from all the four corners of town, using various means to pass the road blocks, which were manned by the Interahamwe militias.

Some gave money to secure safe passage, others used faked identity cards, and still others arrived escorted by born again Christian soldiers, members of our church. Up to the day when the government army vacated the city, born again soldiers were still bringing people they had rescued from the massacres. They could accompany them past the road blocks, presenting them to the militia as members of their own families – wives or relatives. This protected us and all the people at our church, as the soldiers had threatened the militias that they would stop fighting the RPF if their families were bothered. Some soldiers had even gone as far as telling the militias that they would turn on them and kill *them* if anything happened in the church.

All our church buildings and compound were full of people – about 700 – and there was no room left any place. The problem of food was not very acute, as we had stocks of beans and rice that had been bought for distribution to the displaced people from Byumba just months before the beginning of the massacres. The only problem was that the food was stored in a warehouse far from the church where we had taken refuge. So one soldier from our church took a vehicle, went to the stores and brought enough food to last us a long time.

At the beginning we cooked and ate together in age groups: children in their groups and grown-ups in theirs. Those who had money could send for some provisions of things we did not have, such as sugar and salt. But our food stock slowly dwindled, and we were obliged to start fetching food from the market and other places. Those who could go out (the Bahutu) fetched food and those who couldn't (the Batutsi) stayed inside and cooked or did other jobs. Eventually only beans were left, and people shared in small groups: those who had money helped those who did not. Then it became a problem to find water and fuel. One driver from the group ventured as far as Rugunga or Gikondo to fetch water, and we summoned our courage and went to bring wood from Gitarama, although a long distance away.

The militia often visited our place, but they were afraid of taking out people to kill because the born-again soldiers were often there as well. But one day the Interahamwe from the nearest road block came with gendarmes, collected all of us and led us to the military barrack nearby. Only a few people managed to stay behind, hiding in the offices and church rooms. They separated us and took some aside, saying they were going to kill them. We pleaded with them, but they were adamant and asked us to sit on the ground in a muddy puddle, to silence us.

At that very moment one of the born-again soldiers happened to pass by, and he was so angry at the sight of us sitting there that he almost started a fight with the militia. I pleaded with him and his anger soon subsided. They told us to go, saying: 'Take all the other Batutsi you have with you, we will content ourselves with killing these we have taken.' We continued pleading with them, but to no avail. Finally they forced us to leave at gunpoint and we went back to the church, dragging our feet, disheartened. But after a short spell we saw those we had left behind arriving, all safe. We raised our voices in loud praises, thanking the Lord for his intervention on our behalf.

Another day, one of the leaders of the militia came and we were all panic stricken, as we thought this was the end. But he and his escort of killers, all armed with deadly weapons, merely patrolled the place and eventually said: 'These are Christians, leave them alone'. And they left without doing any harm. In fact, the leader later came back with *ibitenge* (wax) clothes, and distributed them among the women and the young girls. We heaved a sigh of relief and praised the Lord again for his wonderful protection and provision.

The previous day, the father of that same man, who was the local administrative officer (*conseiller*), had questioned me. He accused us of hiding RPF soldiers (*inyenzi*) and asked me the number of guns we were hiding in the place. I knew this was done to frighten me, and I prayed in my heart all the time we were together. I told him we were not hiding any soldier and I denied being in possession of guns.

He finally said, 'You church people are like the Red Cross, you can come to the help even of the enemy.'

I answered him, 'Yes, we can do that for any man if he comes to us seeking refuge, not fighting.'

He finally dismissed me with the injunction: 'We, too, are not against charity, but you have to know well who you are taking in. Screen carefully all the people who come to your church.'

Another time they came and besieged the church compound demanding that Pastor Jacques Kayihura, the senior pastor, hand over the keys to all the rooms. He refused. They put a gun on his shoulder and fired, just to frighten him. I then sneaked out to call a sergeant who had promised to intervene any time we had problems. He immediately responded, but we arrived back to find they had all left, taking with them our water vehicle and the church's motorcycles. We praised the Lord again for his protection, as nobody had been harmed.

When the fighting with the RPF became intense, people started leaving the city and we, too, were asked to evacuate people from the church. Some were willing to go, but others refused, because it was so dangerous for them to go through the different road blocks on the way. Pastor Jacques refused to be evacuated. People pleaded with him, but he refused and

34

said: 'These are the children the Lord has given me .
This is the flock the Lord has put under my care.
How can I, a father and a shepherd, leave my children
and the Lord's sheep and go? I will stay with them up
to the end.' So he stayed behind and those who were
ready to go left. I was among those who left. The
vehicle made two trips with people who wanted to go
and we had problems on the check points, as
expected. I had to pay money on the road blocks for
my wife to go through, but we eventually made it to
Cyangugu safely.

Our strength during all the hardships came from
prayer. Every time the threats increased we organised
prayer fasts and we often came out of them strengthened. The people who were at the church were all
mixed – Protestants and Catholics – but we all stayed
together, prayed together and shared everything. The
fellowship was good despite the difference of church.
From the beginning of the massacres until the day
Kigali was captured nobody was killed in our church
compound. We had stayed together and the Lord
protected us.

4 Under the Shadow of the Almighty

Michel Kayitaba & family

> He who dwells in the shelter of the Most High
> will rest in the shadow of the Almighty.
> I will say of the Lord, 'He is my refuge and my
> fortress,
> My God, in whom I trust'.   Psalm 91:1-2

When the plane of the late President Habyarimana was shot down, things did not go wrong immediately in our area, Gikongoro. But there was tension and I decided it was best to set watch overnight. Two Hutu young men in our prayer group joined me; Nyilimanzi, who is still in the camps in Zaire, and Evariste Kamanzi. We shared several night vigils together, taking it in turn to sleep. These two young men showed great courage later when the time came to protect me.

By 9 April we were hearing of people being killed in Kigali and other places, but this had not reached Gikongoro town, at least not to our knowledge. That night, however, Bishop Norman Kayumba of the Anglican Diocese of Kigeme came to my house, accompanied by his wife, one of our pastors in Kigeme and the two young men, Nyilimanzi and

Kamanzi, to 'check if all was right with me', as they put it.

'You see, the political situation is deteriorating very fast. Already many refugees are at Kigeme. Their houses have been looted and set on fire and some people have been killed. It is wise for you, too, to leave this place,' Bishop Norman said.

I was full of doubts at first, but slowly became convinced of the wisdom in their words. We decided Bishop Norman would take my children while my wife and I would go to stay with the pastor. Kamanzi and Nyilimanzi promised they would watch over our house and feed our dog. We thought this was just another of those short-lived massacres, such as Rwanda had sporadically known. We expected things to go back to normal after some two or three days.

Instead, the situation grew worse and very tense, as all around us many people were killed and their homes looted and destroyed. Meanwhile, the two young men faithfully watched over our possessions, and each evening transferred some of our things to the place where we were hiding. Most of our other belongings were hidden at a neighbour's house, so that later when our house was finally looted and destroyed, only things difficult to carry remained anyway. Even then, our two young friends went back to salvage useful building materials like doors, window frames, and electrical wires. They kept them in a safe place, hoping I would use them one day for a new house. (When news came that I had been killed, they gave away some of the things, but others remain, and are still available).

As you can see, these two young men remained faithful despite the threats from the neighbours, as they were regularly reproached with being friends to the 'enemy'. Their faithfulness towards us was not shaken by our hardships and the menace of rejection from their neighbours and relatives. The love of God in their hearts was stronger than the circumstances.

I lived at the pastor's home for some time, until it was found out I was hiding there. I had to move at once, and we decided the best place to go was Bishop Norman's house at Gikongoro. We left that night, and travelled through the bush to avoid the Interahamwe and military patrols. Our only luggage was a sleeping bag and bed cover. We arrived at the compound around midnight, and decided to wait outside until daybreak. So we unrolled the sleeping bag right there in the bush, and laid down to sleep. The dogs from the houses nearby barked loud and fiercely. I guess the owners did not pay much attention to them, as nobody intervened to see why they were barking so fiercely. The dogs approached, sniffed at us, went silent and returned where they had come from.

We slept deeply until day break despite the fear, the cold and the mosquitoes. One extraordinary thing the Lord gave me during those difficult days was peace. One of those days when I was praying I heard the voice of the Lord telling me clearly 'my peace I give unto you because I love you'. That peace remained with me all throughout the rough times, and never abandoned me, even in the face of threatened death.

Next morning we learned Bishop Norman wasn't there in his house. He had transferred to Kigeme, to be near to comfort those who had taken refuge in the diocese. But we stayed on in his house, and soon he came to see us. He kept our two elder children, and left with us only the three younger ones. He also sent some trustworthy Christians to help us, as we could not risk going outside and being seen. The two young men, Kamanzi and Nyilimazi, visited us to bring news of the outside situation, and to comfort us.

Bishop Norman also visited us often, to share with us his worries. He really looked worn out. Then news spread that it had been found out that we were living in that house and we had to move out again. Kamanzi showed again his courage and faithfulness. He came and took us to his own home.

He was a bachelor and shared a small house of 2 rooms with his sister. This lady's children were 'street kids', and followed the killers looting wherever they massacred people. But the Lord kept us safe there, in his small room, with my wife and three children. During the daytime we hardly moved for fear of making a noise and attracting attention. We all slept on a single bed, spent the day on it and used it as a table when we had meals. Kamanzi spent most of his time at home, to be near us in case some emergency occurred.

One day this happened. Some neighbours had come to visit him and were chatting in his compound when our younger son Samuel had cramps from sitting in the same position for a long time and he cried. Everybody must have heard the cry, but Kamanzi took the situation in hand and acted fast. He asked one of his sister's children to go out and see where that child was crying.

Some of the people wondered if the child had not cried from inside the house, but Kamanzi was calm and denied the fact, convincing them it must have been one of those children whose parents had been killed and were left forlorn in the bushes.

'Those innocent children are to be pitied,' he

went on, just to distract their attention. In the meanwhile, we had managed to muffle Samuel and he cried no more. The child they had sent came back and reported not having seen any child around the compound . 'He must have gone to hide again when he saw you,' Kamanzi concluded, to further dampen any remaining doubt in his neighbour's minds. 'What a pity,' he mumbled again.

All this effort was very sacrificial, because if Kamanzi had been discovered he would have paid for it with his own skin. When we discussed this later he told me: 'I decided to keep you here because when I was praying one day the Lord revealed to me that refugees at the church at Murambi would be killed. As you know, this came to pass. The revelation was then from the Lord.' His faith strengthened me, and I felt at peace despite our difficult conditions.

After some days, Kamanzi's sister grew very insecure. All the nearby Tutsi families had been killed, and she kept fearing that if we were discovered, she and her brother would be killed alongside us. So we sent word to Bishop Norman, and asked for help.

He wanted to try to get us into his diocese, to Kigeme. This was a most dangerous endeavour, even for a bishop. Going from Gikongoro to Kigeme was very difficult, as you had to follow the tarmac road through checkpoints controlled by the Interahamwe and extremist soldiers. The roadblock at Gatyazo was the most deadly, and there was no way to avoid passing it. Bishop Norman asked us to consider walking past that road block – he could collect us in his car soon after. But we felt this would be impossible, as we would have to cross the macadam road, with the danger of meeting patrols of the Interahamwe and soldiers.

Finally the bishop gathered his courage and told us to get ready for evacuation at 7 p.m.. We could not imagine what he would do and how he would make it. We prayed and waited patiently. At the given time, he turned up and told us we were going in his car. He opened the boot and, unbelievable as it may sound, he fitted me and my wife inside, locked the boot, and then took our younger son with him on the front seat.

He told the child: 'When we get to the road block, if they ask you anything, say you are my son and you are being taken to the hospital.' We prayed all the way, asking the Lord for safe passage at the road block. Then we got there and the car was stopped. 'The worst has happened,' I told myself as I held my breath, trying to make myself as small and as still as I could.

'What have you got there in the car?,' they asked.

'Nothing,' Bishop Norman answered. 'I'm just taking this son of mine to hospital, he is not well.' We waited for the order to open the boot to come, holding our breath. And then the order came…'Go'. He did not wait to be told twice. We murmured a praise to the Lord and sighed with relief.

The bishop took us to his home near the diocesan premises where he had moved to be near the fugitives he was protecting. Getting into the house was another miracle, as we found soldiers in the front yard, but at some distance from the door.

Bishop Norman went very calmly towards them, as if to greet them. He spent some time chatting very friendly with them, but standing in such a position as to block their view of the parked car. The bishop's wife came and opened the boot for us and we slipped inside the house. When we were well settled inside, Bishop Norman bid good night to the soldiers and came inside as if nothing had happened. We found Bishop Alexis Bilindabagabo, who had also been hidden there.

Bishop Norman decided to go back to his house at Gikongoro, so as not to arouse the curiosity of the militiamen, who could come at any time to search the house. In the days that followed, he spent some nights with us, but when he was not around we tried our best not to make any noise at all, so as not to reveal our presence. We laid down on the floor during the daytime to avoid being seen by any passer-by. Even at night we avoided using any lights.

Two brothers in the Lord from the diocesan secondary school in Kigeme were the only ones who knew of our presence. One was Onesphore Ngabo, the school treasurer, who is now in a camp in Zaire. The other one was Damascene Rubanzabigwi, whose wife Leonilla was discipline supervisor in the school. They brought us food in the uttermost secrecy, as some of the school watchmen had become members of the militia . These watchmen had even killed a man, who, unable to resist hunger, had come out of his hiding place to beg for food. The Lord was good to us, as He had been in other places, and He hid us from their eyes. This type of miracle had become a daily experience, as more than once we lived or passed in the vicinity of the killers without being detected by their vigilance.

Then rumours spread that the bishop's house was sheltering an accomplice of the RPF, who had a radio and communicated with the enemy. This was a way of finding a pretext to accuse Bishop Alexis Birindabagabo. But as Bishop Norman had managed to secure a life protection for him, he did not have to hide and two soldiers had been posted in front of the house to protect him against any attacks. But if the Interahamwe or the soldiers had come to search for the radio as they said, the risk was that they might find us.

So Bishop Norman organised another of those 'commando operations' to get us out of the house without alerting the two soldiers and the watchmen. This time Bishop went out as if to check the car, and opened all the doors wide before going to chat with the soldiers. When the conversation was well animated, we slipped out, crept into the car and waited. Then Bishop came very slowly towards the car singing and talking to himself, closed the doors and drove off without anything being noticed by the soldiers.

Christine Kamunani, a dear sister in the Lord who lived in the village nearby, had agreed to hide us. Bishop Norman arranged for a man of trust to meet us near the road and guide us to her house, so we would not have to ask any neighbours for help. We spent a month and a half with Christine. The experience reminded us of the Bible story of Elijah staying at the house of the widow in Sarepta: we never lacked anything, although Christine was only a poor old lady. Her house was small and did not even have inside doors, which increased the risk in sheltering us, but she welcomed us anyway.

Apart from the danger she was in for hiding 'hunted' people, she had to make many sacrifices to accomodate us. She left her bed and gave it to us as a hiding place and moved across to live and sleep in what would have been the living room in a 'normal' house. She nursed us during all that time, going to the diocese to collect food and coming back to cook for us. We were so much worried about the danger we were putting her in, but she always calmed and comforted us. She always came back with news of our children, who were in the school premises. Bishop Norman had managed to get that place under the protection of the military authorities.

Christine was our only link with the external world. Then she brought terrible news – somehow our presence had again been revealed. We panicked. I told Christine we did not want to be a source of death to her, and we asked her for help to leave for the sake of her personal security.

Christine proved wonderful. She said: 'Think about it, Michel. What would be the testimony I would give if you went out of my house to save my skin, and you were killed in front of my compound. If it is the Lord's will for you to be killed, let the killers come and find you themselves instead of you going out. If then they decide to kill me for having kept you, I'm ready to go with you to death and we will go to heaven together. So, keep your heart at peace.'

I was astonished by such courage and such a spirit of self-sacrifice from my old sister in the Lord – and at first doubted it was more than words. But her behaviour showed she meant what she said, as she went on her normal activities, undisturbed, as if nothing had happened. And then the Lord intervened. Later that same day, Onesphore Ngabo, the treasurer of Kigeme school, arrived to say he was taking us away, as our hiding place had indeed been found out.

'But how can we get out?' we asked. 'This place is surrounded by military trenches.' But Ngabo had brought along some soldiers to help us – and also some good news. Colonel Leanidas Rusatira had come from Kigali with a group of soldiers who did not support the massacres, and he was controlling one part of the area. So we escaped to the area under the control of Colonel Rusatira and his troops. We lived in a house that had been reserved for one of the officers and we praised the Lord for the quick answer He had given, and for the patience Christine had shown in front of danger. Imagine if she had panicked when she learnt that our presence had been found out and if she had obeyed my fears! So the Lord was good to us all throughout and we still praise him for everything.

5 Hunted...Under the Feathers of the Lord

(Jacqueline Mukantabana)

> Surely he will save you from the fowler's snare
> and from the deadly pestilence.
> He will cover you with his feathers,
> and under his wings you will find refuge;
> his faithfulness will be your shield and rampart.
>
> Psalm 91:3-4

The Lord saved me miraculously from 'the mouth of the lion', and it is always a joy for me to testify to what He did for me during the month of April 1994.

On 10 April I was coming from church, chatting with a friend, when I looked ahead to our village, Mwasa. I saw houses on fire and dozens of people running, armed with clubs. I was very frightened. One person we met explained that the crowd was hunting for Tutsi, and killing them.

I immediately ran into the house of Pancrace Kanyamukenke, a brother in Christ, and member of our church. I hid there and Pancrace and his wife Mary kept me informed of what was happening outside. Soon their news became a list of the names of people I knew – who had been caught and killed. But Pancrace and Mary also comforted and strengthened me. I had my Bible and my hymn book, and although I was very threatened, I kept praying.

As the days went by, Pancrace and Mary kept me company as much as they could, sustaining me by their presence, their prayers and sharing the word of God. We developed the habit of choosing randomly a biblical passage as guidance for prayer, and I remember one day when I was very afraid I drew this passage: 'Ask for whatever you want me to give you.' (1 Kings 3:5). This word encouraged me and I prayed asking 'Lord, be gracious and save me from the nailed clubs I have seen those people carrying. But if it be your will that I die that death, keep me from sinning against you before I die.' And the Lord kept his promise, giving me everything I had asked for.

With every day came reports of members of my family who had been discovered and killed, but Pancrace and Mary always comforted me, exhorting me to keep courage and to stand firm in the Lord. But soon villagers who had seen me going into that house denounced my presence to the Interahamwe, who immediately organised an attack. Pancrace went out to meet them and Mary stayed near the place where I was hiding, praying. Very fortunately Pancrace managed to persuade them to leave, but they threatened to come back the following morning.

So when night had fallen I crept out to hide in a thick bush nearby. It was a very rainy time, and each day I spent in the bush I was soaked wet to the bone. Pancrace and Mary kept coming to visit me in secret, bringing me food and comfort. But the search for me grew more systematic, and the rain and the cold were getting beyond what my body could bear. We finally agreed it was best I went to the church at Hanika, where many other people had taken refuge.

In normal times it is an hour's walk, but because I went by night, and had to avoid frequented paths and roads, it took me much longer. I arrived to find a scene of horror – most of the refugees who had been hiding in the church had just been killed – and the few survivors were badly wounded and groaning pitifully. I was terrified and fled all the way back to Mwasa, to Pancrace's house.

I told them what I had found at Hanika, that the people had all been massacred. Pancrace was in a dilemma, as his home was now under close surveylance and would be thoroughly searched at regular intervals. So I decided to leave again that very night for Kirambo, where one of my aunts lived. I hoped to find refuge in her home, because she was married to a Hutu. The walk would take five hours in normal circumstances, but it took me far more because I was so tired and frightened, and had to avoid the paths and roads so as not to run into the road patrols of the killers.

I arrived at Kirambo just before sunrise. My aunt was glad to see me but also was worried because she, too, was under threat. My cousins – her sons – hid us both, but after a week our presence was discovered. One cousin helped me to run away but I had nowhere to go, so I returned the way I had come. I learned later that the killers came and searched his house and when they failed to find me, they gave him a hoe and ordered him to dig his own grave. He dug the hole, but some of his relatives came and so pleaded for him that he was released.

I went to…Pancrace's house again! This time he was really scared when he saw me .'Try to find another place where you can hide before they know you are back. This place is no longer safe for anybody. If they find you here, we are all dead.'

I immediately left and sought refuge with another Christian friend called Beata Kabanyana, a real woman of prayer. Beata was overjoyed and welcomed me into her house. She laid hands on my head and prayed for me, and I felt peace coming back into my heart. I spent two weeks there, and Beata did everything to hide my presence. I could not go out – and you understand all she had to bear with for my comfort. Then somehow the Interahamwe again found out about me, and came to search for me. This time they found me. They took me out during that night, stripped me naked, and dragged me away, saying the best way to kill me would be to crucify me, because I had told them I was a Christian.

I despaired of escaping death, and asked them for a time of prayer before being killed. They laughed and scorned me, but one man in the group asked them to let me pray. I knelt down, prayed and when I had finished the same man asked which church I was from. I explained I was from the Pentecostal church of Mwasa. He took me aside, some metres from the other men, telling them not to follow him. He told me, as if sharing a real secret, that he, too, was a Christian from the Pentecostal church in a nearby village. I was dumbfounded.

He said: 'That is why I am going to do you a favour, if you make things easy for me. Let me have sex with you without much struggle, in a pleasant, friendly manner, and instead of killing you, I will let you go safe'.

I gathered all my courage and told him: 'I would prefer to die than to defile myself to save this body.' Then he caught my arms and started trying to force

49

me onto the ground. I struggled with him with all my might. I was determined to make him angry enough to kill me before he could achieve his other aim. I felt my strength slowly ebbing away, but I kept fighting him and praying in my heart.

All of a sudden he released his grip and told me angrily: 'Go, you dirty girl'. I thanked him. I could not believe he had given up, but he did not make any other attempt to catch me. He went and told the others that he had decided to let me go because I had told him I was a Christian. They brought me my clothes and told me to go, but somewhere else, not to Beata's place. 'Go to another place, far away from here, we don't want your blood on our hands.'

I went, but soon crept into a bush nearby to rest. My body was bruised all over and my muscles were aching terribly. Around 4 a.m. I dragged myself back to Beata's house. She was overjoyed to see me alive and we praised the Lord for his protection. I told her of the miracle the Lord had performed for me and again we exploded into praise. I spent some days with her but we finally decided it was not safe for both of us that I stay. So I left by night and went to seek refuge with another Christian friend called Tamar Twagirayesu.

Tamar was also from our church, and she welcomed me, hiding me away even from her father and stepmother. I spent some days in her little room but we finally decided it was safer to go into her brother's house nearby. I spent the next four days there, but we knew this hiding place would also be soon discovered. I took time to fast and pray, asking the Lord for guidance as to what I should do. Tamar was worried because I was physically weak, but I spent a whole day in prayer.

Then I saw in a dream a large lake, and I saw

myself crossing it and landing on the other shore. I recounted the vision to Tamar and the other brethren who regularly came to comfort me in secret, and we waited to see how the Lord would make it come true. Then we learnt that our Pastor, Fabien Nzabagurira, had been helping people to escape through Lake Kivu, getting them across to Idjwi Island. I asked Tamar to write to him, informing him of my presence, and inquiring if he could do something to help me cross over.

The pastor sent back the message that I should try to get to his home at Tyazo, preferably by night. Soon, Beata and another young Christian called Marcel Subukino came to inform me that a boat had been found to take us to Idjwi Island. I spent that whole day in prayer, praising the Lord and waiting for the night to leave. Other Christians who knew of my presence in that family came secretly to bid me farewell. We took time to praise the Lord for his protection and providence and they committed me into his hands for a safe journey. 'Go in peace, and may the Lord see you off. If we don't meet again on earth, let's meet in heaven.'

They left and I waited for the night to be dark enough to leave. Beata wanted to accompany me because it was very dark, but I told her the Lord would be my escort and I finally managed to convince her to stay. I left Mwasa alone, went by Kirambo where my cousins lived, told them where I was going and they accompanied me to Tyazo, where our pastor's home was. We passed by one road block but those who were on the night shift did not see us. When we got near my destination my cousins decided to go back and I continued alone. I passed another road block and again they did not see me, despite the great fire they had lit. Then I remembered the verse 'He will cover you with his feathers, and under his wings you will find refuge...' (Psalm 91:4).

I arrived safely at the pastor's house around 2 or 3 a.m., and I found him still awake, seated, waiting for my arrival. Another young girl, Tabita Mukandoli, had also come to be helped across. We sat and praised the Lord, recounting all the miracles we had lived through those past days. Day broke while we were still talking, mixing tears of joy with endless praises to God for his goodness towards us. Our pastor was beyond himself, crying with joy as we told him all that the Lord had done for us.

We spent the day there, waiting for the sailor who was to come at nightfall. Evening came and it was time to leave. Our pastor prayed for us and sent us away with a blessing. 'May the Lord see you off to your destination. I hope we will see each other again before long. Don't ever forget all the good things and the miracles you have seen with your own eyes.' He wrote an introduction for us to give to the pastors of the church at Idjwi, and his younger brother Felicien Munyangeyo accompanied us to the island.

We crossed safely and we went straight to the church at Idjwi. We gave the introduction to the church leaders, and had a warm welcome. Although we could not speak Kiswahili or Mashi, the local languages, we found some people who could understand Kinyarwanda, and they interpretated for us. All were amazed to hear what the Lord had done for us, and were pleased to learn there were still men of God who had not betrayed their faith, and were even ready to sacrifice their own safety for the survival of brethren. We stayed with them until the end of the war and then we came back home.

6 *Pastored by the Sheep*

(Assiel Ngwije)

> A thousand may fall at your side,
> ten thousand at your right hand,
> but it will not come near you.   Psalm 91:7

I was pastoring the Free Methodist Church of Yove in Commune Kirambo, Prefecture Cyangugu, when the genocide began in our area on 9 April. My family and I decided to go into hiding. We first took refuge with many hundreds of others in a church at Hanika in Commune Gatare. The killers found us there and started throwing grenades among us.

People fell all around me. Those who tried to escape were caught and killed around the building. Even those who managed to get to the dispensary nearby were pursued there and killed. Slaughter had become like a game to these people; there was not any sense of pity for human suffering. In the end, only a few of us managed to escape, and more than two thousand people perished in that place.

The experience was very traumatising, but the Lord strengthened me and all that time I worked to strengthen the people around me, exhorting them to turn to the Lord in repentance. Life on this earth was no longer hoped for by any of us, so there was a widespread feeling that we had better prepare for eternal life. I led more to the Lord in those two days than I ever have or ever will do in all my ministry.

Meanwhile, my wife and I and three of our children were among the lucky ones. (All our other children had been scattered and we did not know if they were alive or dead.) The five of us managed to escape the killers on 11 April and we went into hiding. We were not to feel the heat of the sun again until 2 June. First we fled to Gatare, where we spent two weeks hiding with two other refugees in the house of an old woman called Bertha. Bertha was very kind to us, feeding us and doing everything for us as we could not go out.

After two weeks our hiding place was found out. We got word that the killers would be coming for us any time. We decided to flee back to Yove, where we used to live. It was easier for us to seek a hiding place among people we knew well. It was only by night that we changed places. We went to the house of Joel, a real committed man of God, and he agreed to hide us. It was there that news came to us that our first born son, who had just finished his studies, had been killed, as well as three other sons. We also learnt that our house had been destroyed, all our possessions looted but that some of our congregation had managed to secure some clothes. We made small bundles of those and sat waiting for the time to move.

Three days later, news came that our presence was suspected and that the house would soon be searched. That very night we left for Mutuntu, and the house of Zachariah, one of our evangelists. We spent eight days there, but as Zechariah had not participated in looting or killing, the killers did not trust him and kept an open eye on him. After eight days we left and went to the house of John, another catechist of our church.

We arrived just before 5 in the morning, but John and his wife were not there. We were welcomed by their children, who were so overjoyed to see us that they inadvertently spread news of our presence. People had been told we were dead, and many of our Christian friends rejoiced when they heard we were alive. However, when John and his wife arrived that evening they warned us that their home was no longer safe for us. So by 8 p.m. we were on our way to Cyato, to hide with Nicodeme, another catechist of our church.

Very unfortunately, we discovered that his house was near a market, and the chances were that we would be discovered at once. So Nicodeme arranged for us to stay with another catechist called Damien Bazibaza. We stayed several days, during which time the senior pastor of our District, Michel Wakana, had been told of my whereabouts and could send money to help pay for our keep.

Days passed, the massacres continued, and we feared the militiamen would finally learn of our presence and catch us unawares. It was decided that the safest thing to do was to get us over to Idjwi Island in Zaire. So two of our catechists, Ephraim Kimonyo and James Turikunkiko, arranged for a boat and sailors to get us across. We went by night, as usual, and reached the lakeside by 1 a.m. We climbed into the boat and set sail. Then, in the middle of the lake, a gale blew up against us and we despaired of surviving. We had been thanking the Lord for his rescue from the machetes, clubs and grenades, but here we were, buffeted by the wind in the middle of the lake, far from any source of help.

Then I remembered the words of the Psalmist: 'I lift up my eyes to the hills – where does my help come from? My help comes from the Lord, the Maker of heaven and earth.' (Psalm 121:1) We prayed more intently and even made a vow to the Lord, of serving him with all our might if we were saved from death by water. By 5 a.m. the boat was landing safely on the shoreline. We sat there on the beach, shivering with cold, waiting for the sun to rise to find someone and ask for directions.

We were led to a local Christian called Elijah, who was holding a prayer group meeting at his house that very morning. They welcomed us warmly, prayed for us and invited us to rest. More people arrived at his house, and we felt bewildered and frightened. We confessed that we feared there might be killers among them. At this, Elijah and his friends comforted us, and told us there were no killers and no harm could come to us in their place. This was 2 June and it was the first time since 11 April, when we went into hiding, that we were speaking to people in a normal voice without having to murmur. It was the first time that we could feel the heat of the sun. We felt like we were being reborn. The pastor of the church came also to see us and asked me and my wife to come and stay with him while our children stayed with Elijah's family.

Two weeks later I went down to Bukavu. I wanted to get in touch with the pastors who were still in Rwanda. I also hoped to find a house for my family there. I was well received by the Christians, and even promised a place to stay. When I went back for my family, there was more good news. One of our lost children, our daughter, had just arrived. She had been found and hidden by one of our catechists,

Sezibera, and two Christian ladies, Maria Nyiramparirwa and Rebecca Nyirangirabami. They had later helped her flee until she caught up with us at Idjwi Island. Her story was an odyssey of its own, as more than once she had been rescued from the hands of the killers.

We moved to Bukavu and soon other refugees began arriving in great numbers. Then I saw among the new refugees some of the killers who had massacred people in my presence. I was afraid they might kill us and did not know what to do. We finally decided to go back to Rwanda. André Ntambabaro, one of our pastors still in Rwanda agreed to come and wait for us at Rusizi river and help us back into Rwanda.

So on 30 August my wife and I and our four children returned to settle in Kigali, because we didn't dare go back to our own home village. Since then, we have been in touch with all the people who helped us, and we are still praising the Lord for his goodness unto us.

7   United for Life

(Epimaque Munyeragwe and Wife)

> For this reason a man will leave his father and
> mother and be united to his wife, and the two will
> become one flesh. So they are no longer two, but
> one. Therefore what God has joined together, let
> man not separate.   Matthew 19:5-6

The killings here in the Bugesera area started just
after the death of President Habyarimana. In fact,
they had started earlier, as there had been many mur-
ders here since the beginning of the war in 1990.
During that time I lost many members of my
extended family, because my wife is of the Tutsi ethnic group.

Although I am a Muhutu, the extremists had me
on their black list, because during the great 1992
massacres I had hidden many people and refused to
give up my wife to be killed. Also, most of our church
members were Tutsi, and my praying and socialising
with them during those days had made me seem a
traitor and an accomplice of the RPF, as all the
Batutsi were considered.

So when the massacres of 1994 started that April,
I was among those targetted . My home was attacked
more than ten times. I cannot go into details about

every attack I had to face, but it was a very threatening time for me, except I had put my trust in the Lord and He saw us through those difficult times.

The first attack came on Monday 11 April, four days after the death of the President. I was at a neighbour's house when I was warned that a gang of killers was headed for my home. I hurried there, and found them already in the compound. They first spoke to me amicably , explaining that we had to get rid of all the Batutsi, because they were helping the 'enemy' of the nation. They recounted stories of those who had killed their wives with their own hands, told of this and that neighbour who had killed his friends, and then concluded saying: 'We know your wife is of the Tutsi group. Bring her out and chop her to death. Here is a machete if you don't have one of your own'.

Such an evil was impossible for me to imagine, but when they went on insisting, I realised they meant what they said. *My* wife had taken refuge inside *my* house and they were asking *me* to bring her out and slaughter her. I made a silent prayer, gathered my courage and told them: 'I will not kill my wife, I will not take her out of the house and if you are determined to kill her, start with me. Here are my six children, start with the elder one, kill all of them and then kill me last before you enter and bring out my wife to kill her.'

They pressed me hard, but I resisted. Then they threatened to go inside and bring her out themselves.

'No one will ever enter this house and bring out my wife while I still have breath in this body,' I told them, with courage I did not feel inside. I knew they could and probably would kill me. We were still hotly arguing when other neighbours arrived, among them one of my brothers and my father. The animosity of the killers receded for a while, and I took the opportunity to draw their leader aside and try and negotiate with him. 'Why are you doing this? What do you get out of killing innocent neighbours? If there is anything I can give you, tell me. I will give all you want but do not kill anybody in my home,' I entreated him.

'Give me ten thousand francs,' he answered. But money was scarce.

I replied, 'You know well the difficult times we are all faced with; where do you think I would get such an amount of money?'

'How much are you offering?" he went on.

"I will give you two thousand and you take away your gang,' I replied.

'Bring five thousand,' he countered.

So I hurried inside the house, reassured my wife, collected all the money we had saved, and returned to where they were waiting.

'Here is all my money,' I told the leader. 'Take it and take away your men, and if you are not satisfied, take it and kill us. We are in your power, you can do with us whatever you decide.'

The gang started shouting all together: 'Let's go, let's go. This is a man of God anyway, and there is no harm from him.' As they were leaving I asked them to give me a paper to certify they had been at my home, so that those who would come later would not harm us. They laughed at my naivety and said: 'Money or no money, she will die. Or find another place to hide her.'

They left. The children were squeezed together around me, crying and trembling. I felt fear and despair grabbing me, but I forced myself to stop and pray and get control of my feelings. Then I went inside to comfort my wife. She had a small baby and was being forced into fleeing. In the days that followed, she moved about a lot, sometimes staying hidden in our home, or in a neighbour's house, or even in the bushes when danger was very near.

Attacks continued on our house all that time, and one almost took our lives. One day a gang of around fifty killers came with guns and machetes, determined to finish with me. But then their attention switched to my motorcycle, and some wanted to simply steal that and go. Their leader disagreed: 'We should have killed this man and his wife long ago. Motorcycle or no motorcycle, our mission today is to finish with him.' He waved the gun he held in his hand.

Incredibly, some members of the gang pleaded for me. 'But this man has done no wrong, he has even been good to us. Why kill him? Let's take the motorcycle and leave him alone.'

The leader was adamant. 'Good or no good, my decision is that this man must die'. So they dragged me out and made me sit in the compound. The leader cocked his gun, took up a firing position, and told his men to step aside. Still one of them intervened, and insisted he first ask me some questions.

'Where are the people you've been hiding? How many of them do you have?' I kept quiet.

The leader was impatient. 'Why ask him questions? We came to kill him.' But the others went on asking questions and finally he joined in, and demanded money.

'I don't have any money left,' I told them. 'But you can take my cow and eat it.' They laughed. Meat at that time had no real value as so many cows, goats and sheep had been left behind or stolen that their value had dropped. Then a miracle happened. All of a sudden the man who had been first to question me said: 'I'm going to lend you money, you will pay it back later. Bail yourself.' I took the money, gave it back to him and they all left.

I stayed behind, full of astonishment at the power of the Lord. My wife and other people I had been protecting were still fugitives in hiding, visiting our home only at night to eat. We had dug a hole to hide some of them; others were in the bushes. I was under suspicion and our house was regularly searched. Most of the people I hid were people belonging to our prayer group and they are still alive. We have much to thank God for, He has been gracious to us during those times of danger.

That is why we came through all this with even more determination to serve Him. In Rwanda today many people are angry, thinking of nothing but revenge. But when I remember how the Lord has protected us, I cannot harbour revenge. I know the people who took my money, I know those who ate my cows, but I don't keep any grudge against them in my heart. I will not even go to court to denounce them. This would anger the Lord, who has protected me all that time...Our Lord taught 'to forgive and to love our enemies', and that's what He expects from us these days.

If the authorities catch those killers and looters and decide to punish them, that's their duty, but it is not right for me to keep rancour. If I were the only person they have offended I would even forgive them publicly and live at peace with them, but they have offended many people and not all have received grace to forgive them. Only those who trust and obey God will be enabled to forgive in that manner; unconditionally.

8 Smuggler of Men

(David Libanje)

> Not to us, O Lord, not to us
> but to your name be the glory
> because of your love and faithfulness.

Psalm 115:1

When the genocide broke out we first heard of it as distant rumours. Then one day soon after people began arriving in great numbers at my home. One was a pastor's wife, along with another woman, four young men and five children. They hid in our house that night, but the following day the killers were getting closer, and I decided to move the refugees to a cousin's house.

Hiding them there at first was easier, as not many people visited his house – he was a bachelor. My cousin showed much courage and this strengthened me for the challenge. We cooked the meals at my home and he collected it for the ten people he was hiding. He ignored the risk of being seen carrying food from my home. But soon we learned that our area was next to be searched.

That night we shifted our friends out past the patrols and over to the tool room in the school where I am a teacher. This area had already been searched, so we were confident they would be secure. But the following day, while standing on the hill opposite the school, I saw a group of militiamen heading towards the school.

My heart sank. I did not know what to do but I made this silent prayer: 'Lord, you can still operate miracles. Let your powerful hand be seen today by rescuing your people.' I took my courage with both hands and made for the place, ready to die if need be.

The group had by that time reached the school compound. Some went into the chapel and took out benches while others roamed about. One of them went to the door of the tool room where the people had been hidden. My friends inside heard him struggling with the padlock, about to force it. At that instant another of the gang shouted impatiently: 'Hurry up, let's go. This place has been searched and there is nothing to take away. Let's go find some cows to eat.'

They immediately left and I crouched down by the road, so as not to be seen. The Lord had answered my prayer and I rejoiced inside. I crept away home, determined to help the refugees across to Zaire that very night. At midnight, I sneaked back to the tool room, trembling with apprehension that the killers might have returned during my absence. Fortunately I found them unharmed, but shaking with fear.

I took them back to my home and the following day I hired some trustworthy Christian guides who would help me 'smuggle' them into Zaire. After midnight they came and we accompanied them to Rusizi, going by the place called Nyenzi.

The distance usually takes an hour and a half to walk, but that night it took far longer, because we had children with us, and it was raining heavily. (That was in our favour – because the patrolling rounds had left the road for shelter.) We prayed all the way, asking the Lord to protect us, and He did. Our friends crossed safely and we went back home. This was the first trip but more would follow.

One trip I remember with lots of praise to the Lord is when I had to help a lady called Lauradia. She had arrived from Bugarama with two children. After a week it was discovered that she was hiding at our place. This time we did not flee through Nyenzi but through Ruhoko, at the place called Rukoko. A man had agreed to help them cross the river, but when we arrived at his home at 3 a.m., he said he wanted to go find someone else to help him.

I became suspicious and immediately postponed the trip. I was afraid that he would betray my efforts to help fugitives get to Zaire. Back home I prayed for the Lord to show me another guide. While I was sitting there wondering what to do with Lauradia and her children, a friendly neighbour passed by. While chatting I asked him if he knew how to help people cross the river.

He said 'yes' and I told him I needed his help that very night. I promised to pay for his labour and he agreed. We set out late at night as usual, and it was almost dawn when we arrived near the crossing point. We hid at the house of Pierre Mapoli, evangelist with our church. The following night, at 2 a.m., we crept down to the river, waiting for the sun to rise. I was curious to see how the sailor was going to get them across . He did not have a boat, but had come with a large plastic sugar bag. Then the time came. He put Lauradia in the plastic bag, inflated it and pushed it into the river. He followed the bag into the river, and swam, pushing it along in front until he was on the other bank. He went and came back for the children. All the time, I stayed on the shore praying for safety. When the operation was over, we praised the Lord and we returned home.

When the killings had started I weighed about 70 kg. But in the weeks and months that followed I lost much weight and became so alarmingly skinny that some people started saying I had AIDS. The truth was that I was tormented day and night with concern for the people I was always hiding. I greatly feared seeing them killed either in my home or on our church compound. It would have been a torture for me to see innocent people slaughtered, and that is why I put such effort into saving as many people as I could. In addition to this natural abhorrence of evil, I knew it was the Lord's will to help other people in need.

Eventually the day came when I myself faced death. There were no people at my home and I was on the road when I met a band of Interahamwe militia. One of them caught me by the throat, looked at me intently and held his knife on my heart saying, 'I don't trust this man. Look at his shape, can you trust him? He must die.'

At that time most of the Batutsi had been killed and there were not any left to be killed. The militia had then started screening the Bahutu, choosing those who were tall and of slender frame, and suspecting them of having blood connections with the Batutsi. 'We must kill all the Batutsi and anybody who in one way or another might be related to them,' he went on commenting.

In silent prayer I committed my life to the Lord and then pleaded for mercy with the group. The man took me down the road into the bush but the others intervened and I was allowed to go. I went home praising the Lord once again for his protection.

I always look back to those days with praise to the Lord. I have seen Him working wonders and whenever I give my testimony I would like all the glory and praise to go to the Lord. We have been his tools in helping those people, but the work was really his. Supposing we had been caught in the exercise? We had no power either to save ourselves or the people we were trying to rescue. Glory be to God alone!

9   No Hutu, No Tutsi in Christ Jesus

Rev. Stanislas Hamuri

> Here there is no Greek or Jew, circumcised or
> uncircumcised, barbarian, Scythian, slave or free,
> but Christ is all and is in all.   Colossians 3:11

The massacres started so suddenly that they took us
unawares. On Friday 8 April a young girl, and member of my congregation, rushed into our compound.
She was panting in terror. Her story spilled out
between her sobs – her parents had been massacred
and her brother had just been killed at the church at
Kiziguro, when the militiamen attacked those who
had taken refuge there. The girl looked deeply trau-
matised, and pleaded for refuge. Appalled, I hurried
her inside so she would not be seen by anybody

She had just entered the house when I saw a band
of Interahamwe, armed with machetes and clubs,
coming towards my home. I thought they were coming after her and were going to attack us, but they
passed right by and went their way. No sooner had
they gone than three other people sneaked into my
compound, all quaking with fear. I pushed them
inside the house as well and sat down, trembling, in
front of the door.

Another band of Interahamwe came along, and

greeted me. As they were going on their way, I asked them as naturally as I could what they were doing. Their leader replied: 'We are killing all the Batutsi to avenge our President. We have killed those we found, and now we are hunting down those who escaped. They must all die.'

Stunned, I nodded, and kept quiet after that, as I did not want to attract their attention to myself or my house. After they passed out of sight, some more terrified people crept into my compound. By the end of the day there were 15 people altogether taking refuge in my house. Among them was our evangelist, Telesphore Kalinamaryo and six of his children. With my regular family, we now numbered 24 in all.

I was determined in my heart that I would never turn anybody over to the Interahamwe. And I would not refuse anyone who came seeking refuge at my home, despite the great number already welcomed, and despite the threats of retaliation the Interahamwe had made against anyone found hiding people. It was my conviction that people should not be killed for their ethnic origins, and I had often taught my congregation that when you are in Christ, there is no Muhutu or Mututsi, man or woman, but simply children of God, all equal.

So in the days that followed, the 24 of us stayed together in my little house, sharing the little we had, and the Lord protected us during all that time. The militiamen continued their manhunt, sometimes even coming to my house, but they never thought of searching it. Then one day one of their leaders came and sat with me in the living room. He started asking where our evangelist Telesphore Kalinamaryo and his family were. I felt fear inside, thinking I had been found out. But I kept a calm countenance and denied knowing where they were hiding. He believed it, and left. We daily praised the Lord for his protection and providence, as we were never bothered and we never lacked food despite the great number of people we had to feed.

A week or so after the leader's visit, we saw great crowds of people running in the distance. They were in disarray and great distress. We discovered they were fleeing from the RPF, who were on their way to the area, vowing to kill all the Bahutu. I discussed the situation with the people hiding in my house, and we all decided it was best to run away as well. But one of my refugees was very weak, having hardly survived the blows of the Interahamwe, who had left him for dead. We discussed our perilous situation with him, and he agreed to stay on alone..

The militiamen were also running away, faster than anybody else! We had not gone far when news came that the RPF had said that everybody caught running away would be killed; that all people should go back to their homes. We consulted again, and decided to go back home. We returned and two days later, soldiers of the RPF arrived. They found the refugees, inquired how all those people had survived the massacres, and were informed they had all been hiding in my house.

We were then told to go and join others in the camp for displaced people. The soldiers explained it was necessary to keep tight control on the villages as they searched for government soldiers and armed militiamen. So we took what we could carry and left for the camp, where we stayed until the end of the war. Then we were told we could go back home.

10 The Power of Prayer

Protogene Dusengemungu

> ...who through faith conquered kingdoms,
> administered justice, and gained what was
> promised; who shut the mouths of lions, quenched
> the fury of flames, and escaped the edge of the
> sword; whose weakness was turned to strength;
> and who became powerful in battle and routed
> foreign armies.   Hebrews 11:33-34

April to July 1994 was a very trying and tiring time
for us local Christian leaders. When the massacres
started, many people took refuge at my church compound at Nyabisindu, while others went on to the different schools at Kabgayi, where there was enough
space to accommodate a large number of people.

When people started flocking into our church
compound, the first thing we did was to organise the
members of our congregation to collect food items
such as sweet potatoes, cabbages, and flour. We even
managed to find clothing for refugees who'd escaped
without their clothes. The number of refugees grew
larger day by day, and soon our compound became
more like a Christian convention than a displaced
people's camp. When the evening meal was over, we

always gathered to praise the Lord and to share the word of God.

Meanwhile, the political situation continued to deteriorate all over the country. Finally the day came when the municipal authorities dispersed the people in our compound, saying that only places under their direct control should be used as camps. Our people were at first reluctant to go, because they were more at ease in our church compound. But in the end they had to comply with orders from the authorities. So they dispersed to Gitarama and Kabgayi – many were later massacred there. We continued to help here and there as much as we could, but it was difficult as the numbers of refugees were now so numerous, and the pressures had grown more intense. We continued to help on an individual basis, though.

This was when I began hiding people in my own home. The first were four sisters in the Lord who had fled from the violence in Kigali, even before the widespread massacres. Then I met a lady called Regina Majyambere near the stadium at Gitarama, where thousands had gathered. The killers had arrrived, and were selecting victims to be taken out and killed. When I saw her in that predicament, bewildered and frightened, I approached her and said: 'I see you are at a loss as to what to do. Why don't you just come and hide in my house?' She agreed and later on I found out she was a sister in the Lord and we praised God together. These people were later joined by others. Many came and went, but eight stayed on in hiding until the RPF captured this area.

It was not an easy job to protect refugees, as the situation was getting worse all the time. The militamen threatened that whoever was caught hiding an 'enemy' would have his house destroyed and he and his family killed. It also became progressively more difficult to get food .We only managed because I sold things from my shop, and bought whatever we needed. I would go out every day and the people hiding in my home stayed in their hiding places, most of the time in prayer. At times, when the stress and danger were pressing on me, I would join in the intercession to get more strength. News kept coming of people like me who'd been discovered hiding refugees, and it was frightful. I was always afraid my turn might come some day. The killers knew me and knew well that my house was a meeting place for prayer and Bible study, and they would not be likely to ignore me. So I always went around with my ears wide open, waiting to hear of plans to search my home.

Then one day it happened. I was walking along the road and ran into a group of Interahamwe. They told me they would like to come home with me to do some routine 'looking around' in my house. I panicked inside but put on a calm countenance and told them there was no problem.

'Come, let's go,' I told them. 'You may not find me there if you do not come now.' I prayed much in my heart, asking the Lord to strengthen me. Also, I kept pleading with him to hide the people who were in my house. I did not know how He was going to do it, but I trusted him to do something. The group walked some distance towards my home and then when we got in sight of the house one of them said: 'Look, we trust you. We do not have time to waste searching your house. Let's go somewhere else.' The others agreed, and they passed my home and continued their way. I smilingly took leave of them, and entered the house, almost flying, praising the Lord who had blinded their eyes and had thwarted their evil plan.

The brothers and sisters who were hiding in my home spent most of their time praying and fasting, waiting on the Lord and pleading with him. The Lord revealed to us many things, among them that no harm would be done to any among us, and that the political leaders were soon to be removed .Future plans and promises were revealed for some who were present. It was a time of blessing despite the difficulties and worries that were pressing us from every side.

My family was one of my main sources of worry. They saw my helping refugees as 'foolish carelessness', and were terrified of the consequences if I was ever caught. But I stood firm in the Lord, praying for their hearts to be touched and their eyes to be opened to see the power of the One in whom we have put our trust. And the Lord proved to be faithful, as five members of my family have repented, just in the short time after the war. I attribute this to the prayers we addressed to the Lord for them during that time and I take it to be a reward from the Lord.

Prayer has been our main weapon during that time, drawing us nearer to the Lord when things all around us were getting worse. And prayer is still our strength today. We are still pleading with God to heal our country, to bring peace, understanding and real reconciliation.

> I have posted watchmen on your walls, O
> Jerusalem;
> they will never be silent day or night.
> You who call on the Lord,
> give yourselves no rest
> and give him no rest till he establishes Jerusalem
> and makes her the praise of the earth.
>
> Isaiah 62:6-7

11 Faithful Determination

Rev. Daniel Ngayampoze

> But Daniel resolved not to defile himself...
>
> Daniel 1:8

On 7 April I saw people running down the road, cars speeding, and everything in disarray. The manhunt had started. The Interahamwe came all the way from Kabuga, armed with clubs, machetes and often wearing camouflage and other bizarre adornments. Fear followed wherever they went.

My heart told me to stay home and stay quiet. At first I watched as the Interahamwe often passed in front of my compound, searching for the Batutsi, or else leading captives they'd found away to be killed. Then people started to flock into my home in great numbers, members of my congregation as well as non-members. I felt compelled as a pastor to do my best to save as many as I could because I did not see any reason ordinary people I knew to be innocent should be chased down and killed.

So I hid one group in our chapel, and each evening I handed out grass mats for them to sleep on. Meanwhile, I organised some protection. A young man, Jean Pierre Gahebi, and I agreed a plan. He would sit on a vantage point and survey all movements around the church and warn me when the militia were coming our way. Whenever the killers were in the area, I would rush to the church and warn the people, who in turn ran and hid in the bushes down here in the valley of Rugende.

Some other people took refuge in my home, often arriving during the night. By day they hid in the bushes, because I suspected my house to be under close scrutiny. In fact, my house *was* searched several times – but the Lord did miracles and no one under my protection was discovered. Then one day the worst happened and I was taken unawares. The militia arrived while one man called Jean-Paul Mukubu was still in the house. I panicked, but again turned to the Lord and asked for courage and discernment as to what to do.

Jean Paul asked me to let him run away by the back door, but this was not a solution as the whole compound was encircled and there was no way out. And if he was found, it meant death not only for him but also for my whole family. So I convinced him to stay put, and we agreed in a whisper to wait on the Lord, and trust him to get us out of trouble.

I took Jean Paul, placed him in my bed and covered him with a blanket, but in such an inconspicuous way that anybody passing by would not take him for someone hiding. The militias were searching my compound and making a lot of noise, so I went to meet them. I tried my best to appear as natural as possible and when they demanded to see my house, I calmly agreed, and went ahead of them, showing them every room.

I kept praying inside, hoping they would turn away and go without going into my bedroom. But when we got in front of its door one of them said, 'Let's look into your bedroom. Is anybody in there?'

'Oh yes,' I said and opened the door very naturally, trying my best to appear calm.

'And who is that?', the leader of the group asked, looking at the quiet figure in the bed.

'Oh, that is my son. He has been ill and he has a respite now and is sleeping.' I made for the bed, as if to uncover his head and prove I was telling the truth. 'Lord, what if they discover my lie?' I was praying inside.

Then the man turned aside and said: 'Leave him to rest.' Turning to his group, he ordered: 'Let's go, there is nothing in this house.' So they made for the door, disappointed with their unfruitful search and waste of time.

I was jubilant inside, and amazed at the Lord's miraculous intervention. But our safety remained precarious. 'Pastor, we will come another time,' the leader of the group said as they left my compound. When Jean-Paul heard the leader's threat to return, he was terrified, and we agreed he would seek refuge with another member of our church, Samuel Kamuzinzi.

It was not an easy task getting him there. For one thing, there was a road block in front of Samuel's house. So Jean Paul and I approached Samuel's through the bushes and when we were near the house, I left Jean-Paul hiding while I went inside the compound. I found three young men relaxing in the home and asked them why they were not on the roadblock. 'We are doing the night round,' they answered.

'But couldn't someone slip past your roadblock now?,' I asked them.

'Yes, but that would be useless. If they escaped

this one, they would not escape the next,' they answered. Then we spent some time chatting about the whole situation, but they did not suspect I was trying to find out how I could help people escape. Then when they finally left I told Samuel I had brought Jean-Paul.

It did not take me long to persuade him to accept Jean-Paul, although he was afraid of the roadblock in front of his compound, and the frequent visits from the Interahamwe manning the check-point.

Meanwhile, the militias had promised to come back to search my home, and they did. This time I was protecting a lady called Immakulata and her five children, and this time again I was taken unawares. The killers had first searched Imakulata's own home, but the family had fled into the bushes. When she saw the militiamen leave her home and start to search the surroundings, she and her children ran on to my house.

Some of the killers were sure they had seen people coming to my house, others doubted it. But finally they made up their minds to come and search my house again. I went out and met them at the entrance of the compound and greeted them.

'Pastor, bring out the woman who has just taken refuge into your house,' their leader demanded.

'Oh, I saw them running down into the eucalyptus forest down here. They are not in my house,' I lied calmly.

'No, they *are* here in your house. Let's go and search it,' he commanded. So we all walked towards the house. I was praying and trembling inside.

They entered and searched the main house very quickly. They did not find anybody. But my house has an annexe in the backyard, and that's where

Imakulata and the children were hiding. Although the killers knew my home very well, they did not remember to search that part of the compound and they left. I accompanied them to the entrance and I went back praising God for this miraculous intervention.

The Lord was with me all that time , doing miracles not only for people I was trying to hide, but also for those I tried to save at road blocks. I remember one day when I was just strolling outside and had got near the roadblock when a young man called Ntiganzwa was caught there. I knew that young man when I was pastoring the church at Muyumbu, his home village. He had fled to Gasogi the previous day but when he got there he found no refuge, as many people were being killed there that day. So he had turned back and tried to escape another way, but the soldiers manning the roadblock had seen him and they called him back.

He went to them reluctantly, and they started interrogating him in a menacing manner. I feared much for his life, and felt so bad because I knew I could not do much for him. But I prayed for courage and finally made up my mind to intervene. I strolled very calmly up to the road block as if going on my way, and then looked at the young man with feigned astonishment, and greeted him with joy and enthusiasm.

'Do you know this *inyenzi* (coackroach), pastor?' the men at the roadblock asked.

'Yes, I know him very well. He is my son in the Lord, I'm the one who baptised him when I was pastor in Muyumbu where he comes from.'

'He is an *icyitso* (accomplice) and we are going to kill him,' they said matter of factly.

'What has he done to you to deserve death?' I asked.

'Don't feign ignorance pastor, you know well these are the enemies we are here to catch and kill. We are going to kill him here and now.'

I was troubled inside, but I kept praying and mustered all my courage. Then I said: 'If you are going to kill him, kill me with him because I cannot allow you to kill my son in my presence.'

'Then we will have to kill you with him,' their leader told me.

'Go ahead and kill me – but' – and suddenly I grew bold: 'You will *not* kill him under my eyes as long as I still have some breath in this body.' The group was taken aback, and started calming down. They seemed lost for words.

Eventually the leader said, 'Let the young man go, he will not go far anyway. There are other roadblocks on the way.' Then he turned to me and said 'Pastor, we do not want you to call your curse on us, go with your man and let his blood be on other hands than ours.' I thanked them and went away with the young man. He decided to go on his way and I have heard that he is still alive and has become a soldier.

As time went on, and the massacres continued, I became suspect number one for hiding people. Whenever I passed the roadblock they pointed at me and said in some exasperation: 'Here is the pastor who protects the *ibyitso* (accomplices).' Then one day they decided to search my house again. This time they came menacingly, determined to get rid of me. Their leader told me, 'Pastor, you know and we know very well that you have been hiding the *ibyitso* (accomplices). We have been searching for the Batutsi members of your church and we have not found them. *You* are the one who has been hiding them, aren't you? Give them to us now, or you will die in their place,' he added menacingly.

'Search my house and kill them if they are here,' I answered, not knowing what would be the result of my answer.

'You are trying to gain time, but we have found you out. We are going to kill you tomorrow. That's what we have decided.'

I did not really know what to say, but I kept praying in my heart. 'I know one day or another I have to die, from your hands or from something else. I'm not afraid of death, but can you tell me the exact accusation for which I have to die?'

One of the militia came menacingly up to me with his machete. He pressed its cutting edge to my neck and said: 'We should kill you now, but that's postponed for tomorrow.' I read my death in his eyes, and in those grouped round me in the road.

Suddenly a great noise – a sort of low roar – was heard from Rugende valley. The militiamen, startled, sent a messenger to find out what was going on. He rushed back with news that the RPF had reached Rugende, and everybody was running for his life.

The whole atmosphere immediately changed. Those who wanted to kill me took to their heels in great confusion, fleeing for their own lives. That day I also lost contact with the people I had been helping to hide – as they panicked and fled off in all directions as well. So I took my family to Kabuga and we hid there. In the meantime, the militias continued to kill. They attacked people they spotted among the fugitives, even though now they were fellow fugitives from the rapid progress of the RPF soldiers in the area.

I later heard that Mukubu had been found and killed, and that pained me much. Imakulata is still alive but she lost some of her children during the flight.

12 The God of Miracles

Rev. Emmanuel Gasana

> If the Lord had not been on our side -
>   let Israel say -
> if the Lord had not been on our side
>   when men attacked us,
> when their anger flared against us,
>   they would have swallowed us alive...
>
> Psalm 124:1-3

It is always a great joy for me to testify to what the Lord did for us here during the massacres and the war. I have pastored this parish for a long time and I have always seen the hand of the Lord in my life, but even more so during the difficult times, when I saw death threatening both me and the people under my protection.

Since the start of the ethnic divisions I have always preached that there are only two races of human beings: those who obey God and those who obey Satan. What happened in our country has been a confirmation of that. From the time of Abel and Cain these two races have been side by side, and they will always be so until the end of the earth.

The situation in our area became tense near the end of April, when people from Ntongwe started flocking to us. Their houses had been burnt down and the killings had started. On 22 April many took refuge here in our church. We organised a 'welcome' to make them feel at home and we comforted them. We had a good time with them, sharing the word of God and strengthening each other in our faith, so as to be able to face the threats around us. Late that afternoon they were divided into two groups for the night: one group was placed in one of the classrooms while the other stayed in the church building. A few hours later another group of refugees arrived, so we placed them in another classroom.

Later still that same evening, the Interahamwe militia came and demanded that I hand over everyone to be slaughtered.

I asked them *why* those innocent people had to be killed. They said they had strict orders from higher authorities to kill all Batutsi. I told them there were no Batutsi in my church but only 'children of God', and I went on to explain to them my theory of the two races, those who obey God and those who serve the devil.

They became extremely angry with me, but I stood my ground. I told them they would have to kill me before they killed the people the Lord had placed under my protection. They finally left, but with the threat they would come back soon. We spent hours in intense prayer, pleading with the Lord and resisting the devil.

Then around 2:30 a.m. a bigger contingent of Interahamwe arrived on foot, accompanied by two minibuses and a Daihatsu pick-up full of armed people. They pulled up at the playground in front of the church singing *Bene Sebahinzi* – their war song. They were brandishing guns, grenades, axes, nail studded clubs and other weapons that they used in their macabre job .

I hastily consulted my wife and a member of my church and we devised a strategy to rescue the refugees. I left my wife with the keys of the classrooms where the people were hiding. She flew off to open them and send the refugees out quickly to hide in the sorghum fields around about, before the attackers would be aware of what was happening.

The Interahamwe were still singing and making a lot of noise in the playground. I went out to meet them, and to distract their attention while those in the classes discreetly disappeared out into the dark fields. My main worry now was for those in the church building itself. But as we had closed and locked it, and they kept silent, nobody suspected their presence. Meanwhile, the noise of the Interahamwe grew so loud and the tension so great that I doubted of surviving.

'Where are the people you've been hiding?' they shouted arrogantly. 'Where are the *ibyitso* (accomplices) that have taken refuge here? Give them to us or we are going to kill you.' Questions, threats, and orders came at me from every side in total menacing confusion.

All that time I was composed and silent, and praying in my heart, asking the Lord to divert their attention from the church building because it was the only place where people were still hiding and they could be easily found. Then the Interahamwe started menacing me and pushing me towards my house. 'You, too, you must be a Mututsi, even your physical appearance shows it.'

I told them I wasn't and asked them to check my identity card. 'We don't trust your identity card, you've probably falsified it. Your appearance betrays you, you are a Mututsi. Let's go first check in your house and see if you are not hiding people in there.' So we all made for the house and they totally forgot about the church building.

They searched all corners of the house, and very fortunately nobody had taken refuge there. In their disappointment they said 'We *know* you have been hiding people. Give us money to redeem yourself or you will be killed'. I gave them money and they also grabbed all the valuable things they could find in the house. They took them and left in a great noise of threats and abuse. 'We will come back,' they threatened.

On their way out they did not even take time to check in the different buildings. The Lord had operated a great miracle and I was rejoicing inside because our prayers had borne fruit. Sadly, I later learned they had caught a group of fugitives at a roadblock, and seized them in their vehicles. Only two young girls were released, while the others were taken to be killed. I don't know in which place.

From that day on we lived from miracle to miracle. Every day came with new threats and attacks, but the Lord stood by our side and no one was killed from among all the people we had been hiding. Every day the killers came, but one way or another we were warned of their arrival, and the refugees at our church and in our home always managed to hide.

This went on all the time until the RPF soldiers arrived .

One good thing is that no one local in our area took part in the killing, looting or slaughtering of cattle. The Interahamwe who vandalised this area came from other places. So today we are not faced with the problem of suspicion, accusations and imprisonments, as found in other places. Bahutu and the Batutsi have returned to their homes and live together peacefully as before.

13 Good Shepherd

Rev.Fabien Nzabagurira

> David took up this lament concerning Saul and his
> son Jonathan,
> and ordered that the men of Judah be taught this
> lament...
> I grieve for you, Jonathan my brother;
> You were very dear to me.
> Your love for me was wonderful,
> more wonderful than that of women.
>
> 2 Samuel 1:17,26

The war and the killings did not come as a surprise
for us. More than once we had been warned through
prophecies that a bloodshed was coming upon the
land and that some of us had to be ready 'to go
home'.

When the President's plane crashed our church
had just finished a prayer and fasting retreat. The
Lord had repeatedly revealed to us during that retreat
that difficult times were already closing in, and that
many of us were now on the threshold of heaven,
among them my assistant pastor, Thomas Murekezi.
No sooner had the plane crash been anounced than
killing and looting started. The businessmen and the
civil servants were the first targets, and at first we

thought this particular outbreak would be a short-lived incident, targetting only those who had wealth.

We got together as Hutu pastors, who because of our ethnic origins, did not feel targetted by the killers. We decided to go and see the chief of the Commune Kirambo, Mr Mathias Mayira. We told him plans were under way to kill people, and that he should try his best to protect the population and to prevent the bloodshed from spreading wide in his commune.

We received the promise that investigations would be made to discover the source of the insecurity and trouble. Rumours were spreading that there were lists of Hutu people that Batutsi intended to kill, that all Batutsi were enemies of the nation and accomplices of the RPF and therefore should be killed to abort their plan. We took all this as unfounded rumours, as no such plan had been disclosed to anybody.

As the massacres increased we, as Christian pastors, decided to organise ourselves to help our Tutsi brothers and sisters in Christ, as well as any others who came our way. We sent secret deliveries of food to those in hiding. We helped refugees find new hidaways when their whereabouts were suspected. Some came directly to our homes. My house became a transit stop, and up to 15 people have been hidden there at any one time. We put them in cupboards, and even up in the ceiling until we could help them escape to Idjwi Island by night. Many came from long distances like Korwe and Gatare – more than four hours walk away.

We had also organised 'rescue squads' of trust-worthy Christians (there were some in our congregations we could not trust) and they were in constant communication with other Christians all over, mainly those whom we knew were hiding people. Most of the operations, be it for bringing people to us, or helping them across to Idjwi, were done by night. We feared retaliation if our 'treason' was discovered. The threat had been made that anybody found hiding or helping a Tutsi person to escape was an enemy, and would be killed with all his family.

This was a very strong deterrent of goodwill, as many people were afraid of dying. But we continued and most of the people we helped survived. My younger brother had his own boat, and he ferried many people across to Idjwi.When he was not available we paid 8,000 francs per person, and other boatmen would row them across.

Pressure was put on us also to join in on the night vigils and patrol rounds. When I saw the only aim was to track and kill people, I asked for permission not to go because of my pastoral duties. The only time I did go was when we wanted to help one girl called Christine Mukarugomwa and a young man called John Baziga to escape. We dressed Christine as a boy, put a hat on her head, and the three of us set off together for night rounds. We passed the road blocks, and went on towards the Lake. Everybody thought we were on the patrol round, while we were taking our fugitives to cross over to Idjwi.

Of all the times of my life, those months have been the most heartbreaking. Many of my church members were killed, and I often had to step over their corpses on the road. I regularly received reports of those who had been discovered hiding and who had then been killed. Other times, when we took food to friends in hiding places, we found they had been discovered and killed.

One small house church, with 150 members, was

attacked and 110 among them were killed. In another place, 34 Christians were killed together. We found their Bibles and their musical instruments, scattered among the corpses. We buried them and went home. I spent days without eating, as nothing could comfort me from the loss of such dear brothers. We had received the promises and the warnings; I knew my brothers and sisters had gone to join the Lord, but that was not enough to console me of the loss of their fellowship here on earth.

However, as the Bible says, those who sow in tears will reap with joy. During the war we hid people indiscriminately – those who were members of our church as well as those from other churches. How could we ask for denominational identity when someone was asking for refuge or help? And this has resulted in good relationships with people we helped. One day when I was passing near a military position the soldiers asked me my name and I told them. Then they said, 'Are you the pastor who helped John Baziga, one of our colleagues, to escape during the genocide? He recommended you to us as a great man.'

'Yes,' I said, 'he is like my own son.' It was a great encouragement to hear that that young man still remembered the help we gave him – to the point of recommending us to his fellows. Those we helped consider us as friends and even as parents, and some often come to visit us and spend nights at our home. Others who survived are now being helped in rebuilding their houses, and this testimony and the previous one attract many into the church.

Some other people have even decided to join our church. They say that what impressed them was the love we showed indiscriminately to those who came to us during those difficult times. For even after the war, some other people went and looted the houses of refugees who were still in the camps, or those who had been massacred. But the Lord revealed to us this was theft, and we preached against it. Then many repented of their looting, and decided to keep the things safe, to hand them over to the owners when they come back from the camps. We are sure this will be another good testimony.

Some people say church leaders did not protect their sheep, and ran away when they saw the wolves coming. We pastors are discouraged by such comments when we suffered with our people. Derogatory comments do not discourage me for long, though, because the Lord knows what we have done. Anyway, bearing with unjustified attacks is all a part of what a Christian pastor has to put up with while being faithful to the task God has given him. And it is sadly true that there are some church leaders who abandoned their flocks, and even betrayed them. The mistake is to make sweeping generalisations.

There were many who chose to stay with their congregations, even at risk of their own lives. For instance, one of our pastors, Tharcisse Kajyabwami of Tyazo, was almost killed for having hidden people. Although the killers finally overpowered him, broke down the doors of his church and killed the people inside, he tried his best to stand in their way. Some refugees he had hidden in another place managed to escape. And he was not the only brave pastor in the whole country. Many made such sacrifices.

If I could give a message to my country at this time, it would be split into three, for there are three categories of people in Rwanda and each category would have its own message.

First, the killers. I would advise them to repent and to get washed by the blood of Jesus. Even if they have to go through judicial trials and even be condemned, this would affect only the body, but they would save their souls. All they did was out of ignorance, because as Moses said of Israel, 'They are a nation without sense, there is no discernment in them. If only they were wise and would understand this and discern what their end will be!' (Deuteronomy 32:28-29)

Secondly, the survivors of the genocide. My message for them is not to revenge. 'Do not seek revenge or bear a grudge against one of your people, but love your neighbour as yourself...' (Leviticus 19:18). It is the Lord's to avenge, and ours to forgive. This is obviously a very difficult message for someone who has seen all his family massacred, but the fact of having been preserved is enough incentive to push everybody into obeying the Lord more. If we do not repent of hatred, we will commit the same sins, and the anger of God will be on us. 'He who hates his brother is a murderer,' the Bible reminds us.

Christians should be real children of God, and live above ethnic divisions. God created us in his image despite any differences we might display. I have four children of my own and a fifth one I have adopted. They do not look alike or act alike, but they are all my children. And we as leaders, as shepherds of God's flock, we need to be near those people who suffered, who have lost their people and show them love. Let us go out and be their new family.

My last message would be for the country's leaders. Power is given by God for the good of the people. That should be well understood by those in all levels of power, and if they do not walk in righteous ways in their manner of treating people, God will not grant them longevity. God keeps his eyes on the leaders and is perpetually weighing them and discarding those He finds wanting. Let our leaders watch out .

14 The Aftermath of the Tragedy

Reflections from the Mourning Week (April 1-7, 1996)

Sunday evening, March 31.
I drove home late and Jean-Pierre, my adopted son, came to open the gate for me. He kept at a distance when I greeted him, afraid I was going to scold him. He had gone to visit children he used to live with in our Unaccompanied Children's Centre, and he had spent the night there. And he had left without asking for permission either from me or my wife.

My wife had been worried about him even before he left, because for two days beforehand he had been looking depressed and did not take his evening meals. Then he had asked for permission to go see his friends, not from us, but from the housemaid! Now I was worried, and I did not know how to talk to him without scaring him off.

When I had finished parking the car in the garage, I put my arm around his shoulders and asked, 'Jean-Pierre, where have you been?'

'I went to the centre to visit the children there. We had many stories to tell each other and I spent the night,' he answered.

'And who gave you the permission to go?'

'I told Verdiane I was going', he answered . Our

housemaid! He knew it was not the right procedure, but I did not want to put more guilt on him. I wanted to find out what was going wrong inside his 13 year-old heart.

'Jean-Pierre, you haven't been well these past days, is anything going wrong?'

'Nothing,' he said.

'No, Jean-Pierre, tell me the truth. You haven't eaten your evening meals for Thursday and Friday, and then Saturday you left without asking for permission as you usually do. What is it that is bothering you?' He kept quiet for a short time and then he put his back against the wall and started weeping. Between his sobs he asked for forgiveness.

'I apologise for my behaviour. I haven't felt well this whole week as I kept thinking of the coming mourning week. I remembered all my family, my parents, brothers and sisters, how they were all killed and how I survived hiding in that hole for months, before being picked up by the RPF soldiers. I didn't want to go near anybody and I wanted to be alone. I left to join the children at the centre because we could share the same stories.'

All the sadness of this young heart came with such power on me that I couldn't contain my tears. I put my arms around his slender body and prayed for him. I didn't have any words of comfort, as at such moments words are just useless. I asked the Lord to comfort him and to heal his heart, mind and body and to give us the grace to be good parents to him.

When his sobs had stopped we both wiped our faces and we went inside the house, silently. I sat in an armchair and looked at the ceiling, musing at the pain inside the hearts of the 400,000 or so orphaned children in the country. 'How, O Lord, are we going to heal the hearts of these children? How are we going to help them grow into normal citizens, integrated, loved and loving?'. Then I stood up, and switched on the radio to listen to the news – and to try and forget the distress of being faced with a problem you can't solve.

Monday morning, April 1.
As I was driving to work, an old lady standing by the road stopped me, asking for a ride. Two men were standing by her side, probably waiting for a ride, too. I stopped and opened the door for the old lady. The men did not make any move. I made as to wait for them, and was about to ask if they were not coming along too, but they seemed uninterested. I drove off and commented on the fact to the old lady. 'I just wonder why those men did not come with us. They are almost certainly waiting for a ride.'

'Haven't you seen how they look?' the old lady retorted rather forcefully. 'They must be Interahamwe.'

'How did you tell?' I asked her, startled..

'By looking at their faces; they both *look* like Interahamwe,' she went on.

'*Do* Interahamwe have a special look?' I asked, just to probe her mind. She turned around, looked at me very closely and said, 'Do you mean to tell me you can't recognise them?'

'No, I'm afraid I can't!' Then I started lecturing her on not judging people just by their external appearances. She kept quiet for a while, but I could tell she was not convinced.

Then she said, 'I think you are right. But you know, this is the mourning week and remembering my children who have been killed makes me

97

depressed and angry. You see, I'm an old woman. I had grown up children who were looking after me. I had houses. I was well off . But now look at me. I have to work hard to survive and to cater for my many orphaned grandchildren. I don't have enough strength. Forgive me for the words, I'm just angry.'

I felt tears welling up in my eyes but as I'm not supposed to weep in public. (Adult Rwandan men are not supposed to). So I just apologised, and expressed my sympathy and compassion for her. By now we had arrived at her destination, and we said our farewells. As I drove off I kept pondering her words, and I could not get her off my mind for the whole day. 'How will such an old woman cope with the many orphans she has in her care, without strength? What can be done for her? How will her moral and physical needs be catered for?'

'The rabbit in old age is fed by its children' goes a Rwandan proverb, but now most of the 'old rabbits' have to go back and feed themselves – and a multitude of orphaned children. It is not rare today to find an old woman catering for twenty orphans, or a young orphan catering for ten or more other orphans. These are cases we are faced with every day.

Wednesday, April 3.
We closed the office and joined the Anglican church nearby for a whole day of fasting and prayer on behalf of the nation and the church. This is part of a citywide chain of prayer that will last the whole of April.

April is the mourning month for the nation, a time to remember the beginning of the genocide. But we in African Enterprise Rwanda have decided to call upon all the churches in the city to make it a month of fasting and prayer for the healing of the nation.

Our vision is to spend time in prayer, repenting of the sins of our ancestors, of our fathers and of our generation, pleading with the Lord for mercy until He establishes Rwanda, 'and makes it the praise of the earth' (Isaiah 62:7). We confessed and repented of the sins of ethnic selfishness, hatred and bitterness inherited from our fathers. We confessed the failures of the Church in Rwanda, starting with the beginning until our own day. We pleaded for our religious and political leaders, we prayed for healing, restoration and reconciliation.

The day was a great blessing for many, and precious promises for the healing and restoration of the nation were prophesied, as well as an unprecedented revival far greater than the one of the 1930's. But on condition that we repent and turn to the Lord. I left the meeting pleading with the Lord to show us how to be tools of his blessing to the nation.

One of the visions given was that of a stone thrown into a pool, creating enlarging ripples. The interpretation was that a bad stone had been thrown into the pool of Kigali in 1994 and it rippled around the whole nation, spreading destruction. Now this stone of prayer and fasting for the healing of the nation that has been thrown into Kigali should ripple around into a larger wave of great blessing. But the Lord needs foxfires that will spread the fire of intercession around the whole country. We finished the day commissioning each other to be the tools the Lord will use for that end.

Saturday, April 6.

Early in the morning I went with my sister, her husband, my younger brother and two nieces to collect the bones of our cousin James, who was killed during the genocide. We were to take the remains to our native village for proper burial with other members of the family who were killed.

All over the country it is the main activity during the week-end for families that have lost their relatives. Most of the people who were killed were thrown into latrines, into shallow ditches or just into bushes. The procedure is to collect the bones and bury them properly.

Kabera, one of our cousins, had been at the spot early in the morning and had collected the bones into a blanket. He was waiting for us on the side of the road with a small bundle beside him. After the ordinary greetings, he went back, lifted the bundle and put it into the coffin we had in the car.

'Is that small bundle *everything*?' I asked him.

'Yes', he said. 'He had been thrown into a very shallow ditch and all the body was totally decomposed. But I've collected all the bones.' A feeling of heaviness descended on my heart and I looked aside to hide the tears that were churning in my eyes.

'How insignificant human life can be,' my sister who was sitting next to me said quietly. 'Who can believe this small bundle is all that remains of James?'

James had been a very handsome young man and was very much loved in our family. He had come to join our grandmother who lived with us when he was five years old, and we had been brought up together. After 23 years of life together, he was more of a brother than a cousin. He spent most of his free times with us and he was at my home at Easter, just three days before the genocide. We had spent much time together, talking about some of his projects for the future. He was always very optimistic. To think of this small bundle of bones in a blanket as the only remains of his strong body brought heavy gloom over my heart.

Everybody in the car was silent. We drove for a distance and then my sister broke the heavy silence. 'I just wonder how people who don't know the Lord can cope with the anger one feels at such a sight!' I was thinking the same thing. Most of the people in the car were Christian believers, and we turned our conversation towards the grace the Lord gives to bear with such grief.

We reached the village to find people busy digging the mass grave where they would put all the bones to bury them in a proper manner. The grave was near the road and I asked some of the diggers why they had put it so near the road.

'For everybody to see it and remember. This must not be forgotten.' One could feel the tension in his voice. All the others around him kept quiet and went on digging. This was a mixed group, and although they were working together at the task, the resentment of the Batutsi present towards the Bahutu in the group could be sensed in the atmosphere.

I left the group to go into the compound next to the grave where all the remains of the victims in the whole village had been collected. Some had been retrieved from shallow ditches, others from bushes where dogs had eaten the flesh and left the bones scattered. The only things still recognisable as bodies were those that had been dug up from latrines, where they had been piled up.

'Let's get out of this place,' my sister gasped. 'I

can't bear the sight nor the smell.' So we eased our coffin from the car and drove off to visit our old mother, who lives some distance away.

On our way back to Kigali, we passed the burial ground again to see if the digging was over. It was. All we saw were some people seated dejectedly near the remains and sharing the traditional flask of beer. They were all relatives to those…'bones'. One of them was already a bit drunk and unsteady on his legs. He stood up and started talking just out of the blue. 'I don't like this business of burying bones. It makes me so angry and I feel like killing somebody. But laws are laws and we have to give to Caesar what is Caesar's.'

'Laws to bury bones – or not to kill?' I asked, just to push him into more conversation.

'Give Caesar what is Caesar's, I said. Laws not to kill *obviously*.' I remained silent, as I could understand his anger and I did not want to push it further. Some of those 'bones' were all that remained of what used to be his large family. Then I remembered the words my sister had said in the morning: 'How can people cope with this anger without the grace of God?'

That is most probably the greatest challenge the government has been faced with since the stopping of the genocide: preventing this anger from breaking into another genocide. Personal revenges *have* happened, dramatic and violent in certain places. But contained bitterness and anger is what mostly remains today, since the Government took drastic measures to dam the river before it turned into a flood.

Even today, though, some people are still afraid of a 'second genocide', against the Bahutu this time.

But experience has shown that when the leaders at the top do not give the green light, no such thing will happen. Rwanda is still what it was: the masses depend on the leadership to act!

15 Is there Any Hope?

> I lift up my eyes to the hills-
> where does my help come from?
> My help comes from the Lord,
> The Maker of heaven and earth.   Psalm 121:1-2

Orphans and widows. Refugees. Prisoners. Two years after the tragedy, more than 1,500,000 people are still in exile in refugee camps in Zaire, Burundi, Tanzania and elsewhere.

A mixture of criminals and a great majority of innocent people fear to return to a country where the victims of yesterday are the winners of today. They fear reprisals and revenge, despite all the promises of protection from the Government.

More than 60,000 prisoners are in our jails, suspected or convicted of having taken part in the killings. They are waiting for judgement from a judicial system that itself has been totally shattered by the war and the genocide. The system needs to be rehabilitated before the trials can even start.

There is an international tribunal, taking a very long time to judge...who? No one quite knows. Who is responsible? And where are they now? By and large, we believe that the masterminds behind the genocide are safe in countries that protect them and hide them from prosecution.

Meanwhile, angry survivors claim justice as their only consolation from all the misery they have endured. Often, their grievances have gone unheeded for more than 30 years, long before the genocide. Angry refugees have already started acts of destabilisation, infiltrating to plant mines and to kill.

Bitterness, hopelessness, anger, fear, threats of another war, hope, promises of a better future... Rwanda is a melting pot of emotions that confuse every observer. That's the make up of the country we are trying to rebuild. People often ask if this country will ever become normal again and my hope and answer is yes...with the hand of the Lord. 'Where will our help come from? From the Lord, the Maker of heaven and earth.'

My mind often goes back to 1983, when I repented and turned to the Lord. Bitterness and anger were deeply rooted in my soul, and they were the most difficult sins to get rid of. 'Too long have I lived among those who hate peace' (Psalm 120:6) and I had grown up hating them.

When I was five years old my father was butchered in broad daylight, before our very eyes, and left for dead in front of our house. He later on recovered, but was taken once more, and we never saw him again. We don't know how, where and when or by whom he was killed. He was taken by the chief of our commune (county) with many other Batutsi and some suspected Bahutu acccused of supporting the 'enemy' and we were told they had been shot.

We never saw his body, we were never able to bury it. This kept us in a state of suspense for many years, hoping that maybe he had managed to escape and would come back some day. The death of a dear one is very difficult to accept when you have not witnessed it, or at least have evidence like a grave to prove it. I grew up thinking maybe my father was somewhere and would come back. When they talked of his death my young heart and mind could not accept it. Today I can understand many people who feel the same way, because they do not have any evidence of the death of their dear ones.

When I finally came to accept my father's death I turned my anger on all the people I had seen beating my father and looting our possessions. Every time I had a problem I always remembered the massacre scene, and blamed my problem on the people. 'If they had not killed my father, I wouldn't be faced with such a problem,' was my simplified way of thinking.

I grew to hate even their children and I remember I used to persecute one of them who was with me in secondary school. He was far younger and did not even know what his father had done to mine. He could not understand why I hated him and I never took pains to explain.

Then during the massacres of 1972-73 we had to undergo a series of humiliating escapes, spending sleepless nights in hiding, uncertain of the future. I survived the experience, but this added to my list of enemies to hate. The tree of ethnic hatred in my heart was growing branches.

When I finished my university studies I was recruited to be a lecturer at the National University of Rwanda and I started dreaming of a successful career as an intellectual. I had my ambitions and I had even charted the route to achieve them. My dream was to become a great university professor, and I often read the biographies of great intellectuals to learn from them how to achieve my vision.

Then, unexpectedly, a big blow was dealt to my

dream when in 1983, just one year after my rectruitment, I was fired from my position by the Ministry of Higher Education... on the basis of ethnic equilibrium. The university authorities heard my defence – but in vain. The order from on high was that I had to go and I went. With a heavy heart, shattered ambitions and more hatred. Another big root had grown to feed the tree of my ethnic bitterness.

That year marked a turning point in my life: I got converted. I had taken to reading the Bible out of boredom and the more I read the more I got convicted inside that my relationships with God and even with people were not right. It was easy for me to repent of many sins, but giving away my anger and bitterness against all those people who had offended me and my family was most difficult.

But I was constantly confronted with the message of forgiveness and love of our enemies as conditional to being a child of God and having your prayers answered. The fellowship with God was becoming so precious to me that I did not want to jeopardise it by refusing to hand over my anger to God.

Then one day I decided to take the bull by the horns and deal with the matter once for all. I sat in my room, reread all the passages about the matter and decided I was going to comply with the Lord's requirements. I took a day alone and sat to forgive and pray for the Lord's blessing on all the people I hated. I made a list of all their names with all the wrongs each had done to me or to my family. Then I started declaring forgiveness to each, one by one and calling the Lord's blessing on them, their children, their businesses and their relatives.

It was a very painful exercise and I had to do it

again and again. But the result was tremendous. I was released and healed from inside and I no longer felt the gripping pang of bitterness whenever one of the old 'enemies' was mentioned in my presence. Since then, the grace of the Lord has stayed with me and despite the pain I feel at having lost beloved relatives and dear friends, bitterness cannot find harbour in my heart. What I have seen the Lord doing with me, I know He can do for my fellow citizens. That is the anchor of my hope for this, my beloved country.

Antoine Rutayisire
African Evangelistic Enterprise-Rwanda
April 16, 1996.

16 The Roots of Conflict

The Country of a Thousand Hills

The mild climate all throughout the year and the productivity of the soil have led to a great population density. Before the genocide and massacres of 1994 the population was evaluated at 7,500,000 ,the Rwandan refugees in the neighbouring countries not included. In a country where 95% of the population live off agriculture in the countryside , it is not exaggerated to talk of overpopulation. This problem of land and rampant poverty was one of the causes of the genocide for two main reasons. First, The small size of the land has always been used by the successive governments to oppose mass rapatriation of the refugees. 'the country is already too small for those who are inside', but very unfortunately for the future of the country no lasting solution was ever given to the plight of those homeless exiles who after 35 years were still considered foreigners and often resented so by the citizens of the countries where they had taken refuge.

On the other hand, the pressure on land occupation was exploited to incite the Hutu population to massacre their Tutsi neighbours, as this led to possibilities of enlarging the plots of land. And most of the criminals that did the killings were recruited from the poor population and the unemployed youths, who were easy prey to propaganda.

Killing was at times just another opportunity to get things long coveted like mattresses, TV sets, radios, fridges and other luxury articles.

One can say without error that if the population had envisaged that the outcome of the war would be what it has been, many would not have engaged in the killings. Economically and otherwise, the poverty in the camps is far worse than what it was and is on the small farms.

The country of three...groups

Rwanda does not have tribes or even ethnic groups quite like other African countries. The Batutsi, Bahutu and Batwa all speak the same language, have the same culture and live all over the country.

Certain history hypothesis has it that the Batwa were hunters and were the first to occupy the land, the Bahutu supposedly came afterwards and were agriculturalists while the Batutsi came last and were cattleraisers. In a country where famines were frequent, the owners of cows survived better and this later on led to a feudal system where the cow was the means of payment for the work done.

The consequence has been that Batutsi have always been resented as foreign usurpers of Hutu power The interelationship between this economical 'cow' power and the later conquest of the political power is quite obvious and no other explanation can be given for the dominance of the Batutsi (who were numerically inferior to the Bahutu).

The Batutsi had been ruling for centuries at the arrival of the white men .The mututsi king was the all powerful Lord of the country. All the others, Batutsi, Bahutu and Batwa alike were his subordinates and he decided their lives according to his will and favours.

The 1959 social revolution as it came to be known put an end to the Tutsi power in a bloodshed that extended over five years up to 1964. This created a problem of refugees in the neighbouring countries with sporadic skirmishes in unsuccessful attempts to come back by force.

Each attack led to reprisals on Batutsi inside, culminating in the 1972-73 massacres when people were massacred this time without any external attack. The Batutsi were slowly being turned into social scapegoats blamed for every ill in the nation. In the meantime no peaceful solution was encouraged for the repatriation of the refugees despite their regular reclamations.

The problem eventually deteriorated into the 1990 attack from refugees now grouped into a political 'front' with an organised , trained and equipped army. The attack was skillfully exploited by the regime to unify all the Bahutu around it. Anybody who was against Habyarimana and his regime was tagged as an enemy of the Bahutu.

They presented the Batutsi as the common enemy and all the Bahutu as the target of the attack. This worked so successfully that when time came to massacre innocent people it was presented and accepted as self-defence. . The truth is actually that most of the Bahutu did not take part in the massacres but were simply unable to oppose it as will be seen in most of the testimonies in this book.

And where was the Church?

One of the hot topics for discussion today is 'how could such a thing happen in a highly Christianised country?'

The 1991 census showed that 89,6% of the population was Christian, with 62% belonging to the Roman Catholic Church and the rest to the Protestant Churches. In Protestant circles, Rwanda was equally known as the cradle of 'the eastern Africa revival'. For all missionary societies – Catholic and Protestant alike – Rwanda was looked at with some feeling of pride and high sense of achievement .

And so the 1994 tragedy brought such a strong feeling of disappointment, questioning and even rejection What went wrong?

Church and Ethnicity in Rwanda

'The cross in Rwanda came hand in hand with the gun' to quote one African writer. The first missionaries arrived almost at the same time as the German colonisers and they worked hand in hand,

When the German administration was replaced by the Belgians in a League of the Nations mandate around 1916, the missionaries staying behind because the French White Fathers present then were on the side of the winners.

A slow movement that had started in the late 20's when many tutsi dignitaries, sensing the advantages there were in being friends with the white missionaries, had started sending their own children to school and to the Church. The missionaries took it as a godsend without much questioning on the seriousness of the conversions.

The period between 1927 and 1942 marked this progressive conquest of the 'Christian kingdom in the heart of Africa', actualisation of the long dream of the founders of the missionary societies.

Most of the chiefs opted for Christianity not out of conviction and conversion but out of interest: the missionaries had the schools and their fellow administrators had the powers even to demote a king as they had just done with King Musinga (this brought about the culture of nominal Christianity where people get baptised more out of fashion than conviction).

When you read carefully the excerpts of missionary reports, there is no single mention of conversion, repentance, obedience to God's laws; the elation is about 'conversion to European culture and concepts'.

In many circles, going to mass and continuing with the cult of the spirits of the ancestors went side by side; the Christian faith responding to the need of social fashion while the traditional beliefs went on feeding and responding to the deeper fears.

While the Roman Catholic Church was establishing its dream of 'a Christian kingdom in the heart of Africa', one event worth mentioning in the breakthrough accomplished by the Protestant Churches is the break out of what has come to be known as the 'Eastern Africa revival' that started in an Anglican missionary station, Gahini in the East.

This revival, with its strong emphasis on a personal encounter with God, repentance, open confession of sin and commitment to personal morality brought a new move into the arena. The flame bearers of the movement were revivalists like the British missionary Joe Church, the Ugandan Josias Kinuka and the Rwandan Paul Gahunde to name just a few on their 'team'. The new members were called 'abaka' (those with a burning faith) in opposition to the others who were of nominal, dead, cold faith.

The movement touched mainly people at the grassroot level but some nobles and even high ranking chiefs like Ruhorahoza of Bugesera and Mbaraga of Kanage were among the new 'barokore'. The revival had some impact on the ethnic relationships as many Batutsi started humbling themselves and repenting of the arrogance towards other ethnic groups.

The 1959 revolution and its accompanying massacres quenched the fire of the revival before it had produced lasting results on the social and ethnic relationships.

The Protestant Churches, moreover, did not gain ground in the higher spheres of authority and until recently have never managed to be of as much influence as the Roman Catholic Church.

In this given context, it is not astonishing that Rwanda produced a Church that was inefficient when time came to deal with the most crucial problem of ethnicity. The Roman Catholic Church was so enmeshed with the polical powers that all changes went with their 'blessing' and whatever they opposed was condemned to fail.

When Habyarimana took power and massacred Kayibanda and all his dignitaries, another Roman Catholic cleric, Archbishop Vincent Nsengiyumva took over and became the 'spiritual' adviser of the president. He even at one time was elected to sit as member of the Central Committee of the one party MRND, a position he left with some strong pushing from the Vatican. It reads as if the Church has always been leaning on the winner's side whether in the right or wrong. Maybe the present row with the RPF is just the result of disappointment at having miscalculated the opposition.

During the genocide the Church leadership leaned too much on the Government and its army, keeping silent on their executions while being out-spoken on the RPF's , to finally find out that they had sided with the losing side. As someone said in a discussion 'our Church leaders kept quiet when they should speak and spoke when they were supposed to keep quiet'. This is the most probable reason many leaders are still outside the country 'fearing for their own lives' while those who dared to return have not been bothered – as far as their lives are concerned I must hasten to add. Some are now going through rough times in a merciless power struggle and the main argument used against them is none other than the support they gave to the former régimes.

This weakness of the Church as an institution in front of social crises can be explained by various rea-sons. One of the reasons is the close association of Church leadership with politics. This lack of self-dis-tancing from the circles of political influence leads to the muzzling of the prophetic voice in times of crises.

The Eastern Africa Revival gave a different per-spective on the issue and conversion was rightly preached as a prerequisite for being called a real Christian. However, their legacy contained many small flaws that were to lead to the inefficiency of the Christians in times of crises. First,the 'balokole' movement was so heavenly-minded that it forgot that Christianity has duties even here on earth This led to a kind of naive faith, often irrelevant when it came to dealing with social issues.

This was so evident during the 1990-1993 period when some of the Christian organisations started organising informal meetings and even public rallies to think about the Christian social duties and to denounce the evils of the day. The 'evangelical' Christians (born again) often opposed and dismissed the teachings , even when based on the Bible, as political talk . I remember one well meaning dear brother in the Lord who came to me after listening to a talk I had been asked to give on 'the Christian and politics' and who said 'the message was good but you diluted it with politics.'

Another characteristic of the movement as pointed out before was the emphasis put on personal testimony. This is very biblical but the weakness in many of our Church meetings was lack of balance: personal testimonies took greater time than anything else and finally became almost the hallmark of spiritual maturity. This in the long run has led to a very poor Church, with many old people who should be teachers but still needing to be fed on milk...Christian babies only able to give old testimonies of how they got saved somewhere in the 30's!

The lack of biblical teaching is still a weakness in the Church and will be for a long time as people have not been trained to enjoy discussing and sharing the Bible. Preference goes always to preaching, and this is often done so poorly that no solid grounding in the Word of God is provided.

I would like to finish here with a plea for objectivity in relation to one of the criticisms that has been made against the Church , namely that Church buildings became butcheries during the massacres. This is true as more people were killed in Churches than in any other place but this should not be blamed on the Church. Taking refuge in Church buildings had a precedence as in previous massacres anybody who managed to get into a Church was safe. The Church was then respected and venerated as a sacred place.

The novelty of the 1994 genocide is that the killers, who knew of this decided not only to desecrate the Church buildings but also to encourage the victims to flock into those places to make their dirty job easier.

In one place the desecration of the Church and what it represents was so complete that a group of killers put on clerical clothes and went on the road block to bless the killers any time they were about to kill a victim.

In another place, the killers had composed a slogan saying 'the God of the Batutsi is dead and they cannot survive'. No Church leader was armed to confront the well equipped and trained squads of killers and those who tried to resist were killed without any hesitation. Moreover, despite what many people often tend to believe, not many clergymen were directly involved in the killings.

Postscript

Rwanda – a missionary reflects on a catastrophe
The following is an extract from the J. C. Jones Lecture 1995, given by the Rev. Roger Bowen, General Secretary of Mid-Africa Ministry (CMS) – used by permission

Following the catastrophe in Rwanda with between half a million to a million dead, two million as refugees and one million displaced within the country, we are left with many questions. One of the most acute is for the Churches. How could this catastrophe have happened in such a predominantly Christianised country? In the 1991 census 90% of Rwandans called themselves Christians – 62% Catholic, 18% Protestant, 8% Adventist. For Catholic missions which started in the late 19th century, both Rwanda and its neighbour Burundi, were seen as the most successful examples of Catholic mission in Africa. In Rwanda, after the Government, the Catholic Church was the single most powerful institution, being involved in a great variety of educational, medical and social ministries.

The agonising irony of what happened in Rwanda is also felt very acutely by the Protestant Churches, and not least the Anglicans. For many in the Anglican Communion Rwanda was synonymous with a great movement of the Holy Spirit in the 1930s and 1940s which became known as the East African Revival. It swept through the whole of East Africa but many would trace its source to events in both Uganda and Rwanda in the 1930s which brought new life to Protestant Churches throughout the region. How is it, people ask, that Churches marked by such a profound revival, seem to have been drawn into this appalling slaughter, and by and large, have been unable to deal with the ethnic and power issues within the Christian community itself, let alone in the wider society?

In order to situate what happened in April 1994, it is important to sketch in the historical context. Events of such magnitude are always connected to preceding events and it is important to be aware of the world in which the Church in Rwanda existed and the influences that were pressing upon it.

Historical Context

In the colonial carve up of Africa following the Berlin Conference on Colonial Question, in 1884, Rwanda and Burundi became part of German East Africa. They were traditional kingdoms ruled by the minority Tutsi pastoralists while the Hutu majority were largely agriculturalists, and the tiny minority, about 1%, of Batwa pygmies were hunter gatherers. They all shared the same language and culture and the distinctions between the different groups were not rigid. It is said that a Hutu who owns ten or more cows could become a Tutsi. Following the defeat of Germany at the end of the First World War, her territories were shared out amongst the victors. Rwanda and Burundi were given by the League of Nations to

Belgium to administer. Belgium used the traditional structure of Tutsi chiefs to administer the country, but rigidified the ethnic distinction by only educating the sons of Tutsi chiefs. This led to a much more rigid distinction between Tutsi (14%) and Hutu (85%) than had existed previously. In 1959, with imminent independence looming, the Belgian authorities and the Roman Catholic Church switched allegiance from the Tutsi minority to the Hutu majority, bringing about a Hutu revolution and take-over at independence in 1962. Tutsi counter-attacks produced pogroms and many Tutsi fled into exile. It is their sons and daughters who formed the Rwandan Patriotic Front in Uganda which invaded Rwanda in 1990. Their frustration at being in exile and being stateless (they were neither allowed to return to Rwanda nor to take citizenship of the country in which they were exiled), is the background to their invasion.

The Hutu leader of the newly independent Rwanda in 1962 was President Kayibanda who came from the south of the country. The military coup in 1973 which brought Juvenal Habyarimana from the north west of Rwanda to power, revealed the strong power struggle between north and south among the Hutu themselves. Habyarimana began well but gradually he abused his authority until all the positions of power in the country were concentrated in members of his family and a clique, known as the 'akazu', 'the little house', from his home area in the north of the country. This concentration of power, unscrupulously used, was resented by other Rwandans – Hutu and Tutsi alike. The forced introduction of multi-party democracy, the RPF invasion of 1990, the pressure for power-sharing arrangements, were seen as a threat to Habyarimana's monopoly of power.

Morever, the failed coup in Burundi and assassination of a democratically elected Hutu president in 1993 by members of the Tutsi-dominated Burundi Army gave Hutu extremists in Rwanda further ammunition – the Tutsi cannot be trusted and any attempt to share power with them in Rwanda would be suicidal. The aircrash of 6 April 1994, which killed both President Habyarimana and the Burundian President, led the Hutu extremists in Rwanda to unleash their killing machine and final solution for maintaining power. Opposition Hutu groups were targeted and especially ethnic Tutsi, but it is a mistake to see what happened in Rwanda simply as an ethnic conflict. It is essentially about power and the lengths to which a group will go to hang on to its power.

Church and state

'A church too closely identified with a regime shares its fate.' The Roman Catholic Archbishop of Rwanda had sat on the Central Committee of the ruling party of President Habyarimana's government. Some members of the Anglican hierarchy were public supporters of the former President and courted his favour and patronage. There appears to have been little ability to maintain a critical distance vis a vis the governing authorities. The Church hierarchies remained 'too closely linked with the ruling regime to be a credible voice of protest. Their many declarations during the genocide were insignificant and inadequate. Church reaction was too late and too little.' (Fr. W. Schonecke 'What does the Rwanda tragedy say to AMECEA Churches?' AMECEA Documentation Service, Nairobi, Kenya. 17/1994, No. 424.)

From a Protestant perspective, one is bound to ask whether the theological foundations bequeathed to the newly independent African Church by the missionaries were adequate to deal with the Church-State issues.

Injustice and impunity

In Rwanda the lesson had not been learned that unresolved injustice in one generation will return to haunt the next. The Tutsi exiles from the early 1960s had never been allowed back to Rwanda and had remained in exile for thirty years as stateless people. The Church in Rwanda failed to plead their cause perhaps because, in the Anglican Church at least, the leadership was exclusively Hutu... Gross abuses of human rights were taking place within Rwanda long before the crisis of April 1994, yet the Churches by and large did not speak up. There has been a failure to see that abuse of human beings, created in the image of God, is a very serious issue that the Church cannot ignore if it is to be true to its Lord.

The history of Rwanda and Burundi is scarred by outbreaks of appalling ethnic conflict of an horrific nature. In all cases there has never been a bringing to justice of the major perpetrators. A climate of impunity has been created which gives the impression that people can get away with such behaviour without fear of being brought to trial. There is little doubt that the assassination of President Ndadaye of Burundi in October 1993, and the fact that no one had been brought to justice for that event, gave the green light to the Rwandan Government that they too could get away with their genocidal plans without fear of arrest and trial. Prior to the genocide in

Rwanda there had been outbreaks of ethnic violence and considerable abuse of human rights, yet the Churches failed to call for the perpetrators to be brought to justice and for justice to be seen to be done. The climate of impunity created a climate of confidence for those bent on maintaining their power and influence at all costs.

Ethnicity and identity

In many parts of the world today in situations of economic, social or political stress we see people falling back on their ethnic identity with often violent results. In Rwanda in a situation of insecurity and threat caused by the RPF invasion in 1990, by the imposition of Structural Adjustment Programmes leading to high urban unemployment, by the imposition of multi-party politics, and by economic decline, people fell back on their ethnic identity and were encouraged to do so by unscrupulous politicians. Sadly, within the Church itself the mutual fears between Hutu and Tutsi were not faced up to and dealt with. Wi' hin the Anglican Church it was hard for Tutsi to advance in leadership while the hierarchy remained solidly Hutu. The issue which, in the past in times of revival had been addressed so powerfully, was allowed to remain unresolved. The challenge to find a deeper, more fundamental identity 'in Christ' where there is no Jew nor Greek, Hutu or Tutsi, seems to have been forgotten by many. There were glorious exceptions to this...of heroic faith and courage where Christians who were also Hutu helped and protected their Tutsi neighbours from the Interahamwe militias. By and large, however, the Church had allowed these ethnic tensions to continue unresolved, often below the surface, until conditions occurred where the issue exploded beyond their control in horrific violence.

What sort of evangelisation?

Bishop Nsengiyumva (Roman Catholic) of Rwanda said 'The Christian message is not being heard. After a century of evangelisation we have to begin again because the best catechists, those who filled our Churches on Sundays, were the first to go out with machetes in their hands.' (From Richard Dowden, Vocation for Justice, Summer 1994, Vol 8, No 2.) It is a heart cry which is relevant to all the Churches in Rwanda... I am reminded of a comment made to me by a French priest in Burundi, 'we have sacramentalised the Barundi, we have not evangelised them'.

The catastrophe of Rwanda raises the issue of how deeply the Gospel has penetrated both individuals and the culture and what sort of evangelism is needed in order to address the issues that really trouble Africans.

The role of the Media

The catastrophe in Rwanda has raised very sharply the issue of the enormous power and influence of media and disinformation, particularly in a context where the vast majority of listeners are illiterate and have no other means of verifying the truth or falsity of what they are hearing. Both sides in the Rwanda conflict had their radio station. The RPF 'Radio Muhabura' was very successful in communicating to the Western media a righteous image of a well-disciplined army, with a just cause, doing battle with a corrupt and abusive government bent on genocide as a means of maintaining its power. The Rwandan Government used the infamous 'Radio Television Libre Milles Collines' to pump out vicious and racist incitement to 'kill more Tutsis, the graves aren't full enough'. The unscrupulous manipulation of a largely illiterate peasant population was horrifyingly effective...

Land and population

Rwanda was the most densely populated country in Africa. There was a dramatic increase in population from 2.8 million in 1962 to an estimated 7.5 million in 1990, with a density of 285 inhabitants per square kilometre. Scarcity of land is a major issue in the conflict and often, perhaps at subconscious levels, the violence and mass-murder of whole populations has been motivated by a desire for living space. Certainly in a society where the vast majority of the population have to live off the produce of their plot of land, the issues of space and ownership are crucial. The tension is only heightened by the increase in population.